MW01224166

DIVIDEND GROWTH

Freedom Through Passive Income
[Canadian Edition]

By

Mike Heroux

The Dividend Guy

Table of Contents

LEGAL STUFF & ETC.

THE CONTENTS OF THIS MANUAL REFLECT THE AUTHOR'S VIEWS ACQUIRED THROUGH HIS EXPERIENCE ON THE TOPIC UNDER DISCUSSION. THE AUTHOR OR PUBLISHER DISCLAIMS ANY PERSONAL LOSS OR LIABILITY CAUSED BY THE UTILIZATION OF ANY INFORMATION PRESENTED HEREIN. THE AUTHOR IS NOT ENGAGED IN RENDERING ANY LEGAL OR PROFESSIONAL ADVICE. THE SERVICES OF A PROFESSIONAL PERSON ARE RECOMMENDED IF LEGAL ADVICE OR ASSISTANCE IS NEEDED.

WHILE THE SOURCES MENTIONED HEREIN ARE ASSUMED TO BE RELIABLE AT THE TIME OF WRITING, THE AUTHOR AND PUBLISHER, OR THEIR AFFILIATES, ARE NOT RESPONSIBLE FOR THEIR ACTIVITIES. FROM TIME TO TIME, SOURCES MAY TERMINATE OR MOVE AND PRICES MAY CHANGE WITHOUT NOTICE. SOURCES CAN ONLY BE CONFIRMED RELIABLE AT THE TIME OF ORIGINAL PUBLICATION OF THIS MANUAL.

THIS MANUAL IS A GUIDE ONLY AND, AS SUCH, SHOULD BE CONSIDERED SOLELY FOR BASIC INFORMATION. EARNINGS OR PROFITS DERIVED FROM PARTICIPATING IN THE FOLLOWING PROGRAM ARE ENTIRELY GENERATED BY THE AMBITIONS, MOTIVATION, DESIRES, AND ABILITIES OF THE INDIVIDUAL READER.

NO PART OF THIS MANUAL MAY BE ALTERED, COPIED, OR DISTRIBUTED WITHOUT PRIOR WRITTEN PERMISSION OF THE AUTHOR OR PUBLISHER. ALL PRODUCT NAMES, LOGOS, AND TRADEMARKS ARE PROPERTY OF THEIR RESPECTIVE OWNERS WHO HAVE NOT NECESSARILY ENDORSED, SPONSORED, OR APPROVED THIS PUBLICATION. TEXT AND IMAGES AVAILABLE OVER THE INTERNET AND USED IN THIS MANUAL MAY BE SUBJECT TO INTELLECTUAL RIGHTS AND MAY NOT BE COPIED FROM THIS MANUAL.

For Canadians Only, eh! (Because the Loonie is Cooler!)

First things first, **THANK YOU!** If you are reading this book, it means that you have purchased it. I want to thank you for letting me explain my perspective on dividend investing. I feel privileged that we will walk side by side for a moment during your investment journey.

I've put in many hours researching, writing, editing or arguing violently (lol!) with my partner to produce this eBook. After writing the most complete eBook on <u>dividend investing for beginners</u>[1], I'm on my journey to achieve the very same accomplishment for more advanced investors. In this book, I wanted to explore the more technical aspects of dividend investing and delve into the mechanics of building a high dividend yield, low risk portfolio. All this is possible through the power of dividend growth!

This is a "for Canadians only" eBook. This means that all of my examples are taken with Canadian dividend stocks, where I use Canadian dividend stock screeners and Canadian resources. I'm also factoring in **tax implications** ('cause all we do in Canada is pay more and more taxes!), throughout the different strategies shown in this book.

As a Canadian, it was easier for me to understand the complexity of our tax system, combined with the 3 major types of accounts: RRSP (registered retirement saving plan), TFSA (tax-free savings account) and Cash account (non-registered). Our stock market is mainly composed of financials and resources, and most Canadian investors consider investing at least part of their portfolio in the US stock market where dividend stocks are more diversified. Concerns still remain, however, regarding tax implications and currency risks. This

---

[1] http://www.thedividendguyblog.com/2011/06/02/dividend-investing-ebook/

is just one example of the specific topics we will touch on throughout this book. I'm going to answer both these concerns with quick and easy to use guidelines.

I will be writing a "US version" of this book considering their specific investments and strategies as well, in the hopes that everybody will be served ☺. Keep in mind that the strategy might be different for a US investor, as they benefit from a larger and more diversified stock market. If you are Canadian, this is the perfect book for you.

A Little About Me

My name is Mike (like half of the financial bloggers!). I am 30 and married with 3 young kids (William; 6 Amy; 4 and my newborn infant, Caleb). I work in the financial industry (my day job) and I also run an online company with my best friend. Additionally, I am the author behind The Financial Blogger[2] (since 2006) and The Dividend Guy Blog[3] (since August 2010). More recently, I have created 3 unique resources for dividend investors; What Is Dividend?[4], Canadian Dividend Stock[5] and Dividend Stock Analysis[6].

My passion for investing started in 2003. As soon as I signed the contract for my first job, I ran to a nearby bank and opened both a line of credit and a brokerage account. I took all of the money from my line of credit (that was very gutsy!) and started investing in the stock market. Three years later (in 2006), I was buying my first house with a $50,000 down payment (all from my investment profits). This, however, was after making money on several trades on HSE.UN (Harvest Income Trust), GW (Garda World), PDN (Paladin), National Bank (NA), MBT (Manitoba Telecom), POW (Power Corporation) and many others.

---

[2] www.thefinancialblogger.com
[3] www.thedividendguyblog.com
[4] www.whatisdividend.com
[5] www.canadiandividendstock.com
[6] www.dividendstockanalysis.com

Since then, my interest in the financial markets has never stopped growing. In 2008, I became a financial planner in the great region of Montreal, Canada, and I now share my financial knowledge with both my clients and the readers of my blogs.

While I was completing my Certified Financial Planner title along with my MBA in financial services, I started losing track of my investments and lost money with risky trades on NRN (Northern Shields), PDN (Palandin...never fall in love with a stock!) and RIM (Research in (DE)Motion).

In 2010, I bought The Dividend Guy Blog, as I was really interested in dividend investing. Dividend investing requires less time and offers greater potential for investment return than my aggressive way of managing my portfolio. This is how I switched almost all my investments toward a dividend portfolio while authoring this blog twice a week.

In 2011, I launched Dividend Investing – How To Build a Never Ending Cash Distributor[7]. This is a very complete beginner's guide to dividend investing. After 15,458 downloaded copies in 6 months, I've noticed that:

a) I could have made a killing selling this book for $5!
b) My reader's thirst for dividend information will not be satisfied with just one book. I needed to provide a more advanced version. That would be this book!

I knew from the responses to my first book on Dividend Investing that you would be looking for more detailed and complete information. That is why I wrote this second book.

I'll be asking you several questions throughout this book. This is my way of connecting with you while you are becoming the ultimate

---

[7] http://www.thedividendguyblog.com/2011/06/02/dividend-investing-ebook/

dividend investor. I really like to connect with my readers and exchange ideas on different investing topics. I encourage you to sign-up for the Dividend Guy Blog's Free Newsletter[8] in order to stay connected.

So, are you ready to start? Let's do it! Let's start with a question:

Do you have the right book?

This book is for Canadian investors. So if you're not from Canada, a big chunk of this book won't be of any of use to you. II suggest looking for the US version of this book if that is the case.

Please remember that this book is addressed to experienced investors. By "experienced," I don't mean experts or professionals. I want to make sure that you master the basics of investing before you read on. Investing without knowledge is as dangerous as driving a car in winter without your license and winter tires! That is why I want to make sure that you master the following concepts:

➢ *You know your risk tolerance;*
➢ *You know your investor profile;*
➢ *You are familiar with asset allocation principles;*
➢ *You are familiar with most financial ratios (such as P/E ratio, ROE, Debt/Equity ratio, etc);*
➢ *You are familiar with dividend metrics (dividend yield, dividend payout ratio, dividend growth rate, etc.);*
➢ *You have your brokerage account and have already traded a few times.*

If this isn't you, don't panic yet! You didn't buy this book for nothing... BUT you do need to read my first book before tackling these advanced concepts! The good news is that **Dividend Investing is free!** You will find all the necessary information to cover the basics of investing before you reopen this book and start with the more complex stuff. **You can d**ownload my free eBook **from my website:**

---

http://www.thedividendguyblog.com/dividend-investing-ebook/

I'm well aware that the notions of investor profile and risk tolerance are not easy to determine for an investor. For a definition of the most common risk profiles, see this post here:

http://www.thedividendguyblog.com/investment-risk-profiles/

There are a lot of tools on the web to help determine risk profiles, but the one that I prefer is at the TIAA-CREF website[9]. It is quick and gets results:

What you should expect from this book?

If you have seen my sales page for this book, you have read this portion of my book already. I want to make sure, however, that you know what you are buying and why you bought it. This is your journey, so it's important that you know where you're coming from and where you're going.

So this is what you are going to get for your bucks:

- ✓ *Information on how to master the concepts of dividend growth and asset allocation, and how to **receive bigger dividends with less risk;***
- ✓ ***Custom investing strategies** considering the type of accounts (non-registered, TFSA, RRSP) and the amount you have to invest;*
- ✓ ***How not to get fooled by the tax guy**, but instead, learn the implication of US dividend stocks in your portfolio;*
- ✓ *Information on how to stop hesitating on trading your stocks**, and learning the triggers to buy and sell** stocks;*
- ✓ *Knowledge of when to add or remove stocks and which ones to add or remove;*

---

[9] https://ais4.tiaa-cref.org/asstallocguidance/nsjsp/start.do

✓ *Access to a portfolio model example;*

✓ *Information regarding how to seek both capital gains and dividend growth.*

Most importantly:

I'm not a financial guru, but I do have extensive experience investing. You won't get stock recommendations but you will get stocks on my radar list. You won't learn how to make money on the stock market, but you will learn how to invest carefully. You won't become a tax expert, but you will understand the implication of holding US dividend stocks in your different types of accounts.

Finally, you'll get a series of quotations from Oscar Wilde and a few other celebrities (because I find them funny)!

Last Warning: Dividend Investing is Everything but Sexy

Before we go any further, I have to warn you: what you are going to read in this book is not fascinating. It is not intriguing. It is not sexy. In fact, dividend investing is probably one of the most boring investing methods ever! It comes with all kinds of boring requirements:

➢ *Patience, patience and PATIENCE!;*

➢ *Analysis skills (don't worry, we'll develop this together);*

➢ *Low turnover portfolio (equals less trades, equals less adrenaline trading);*

➢ *Great saving habits (to continue to dip into your investing account).*

As you can see, there is nothing very exciting about dividend investing. On top of that, you will never have that crazy story for your Xmas party where you made 142% with your latest trade in the span of 6 months. In reality, you will average 3-4% dividend yield at first and that will not even be enough to overcome the effect of a bear market on your portfolio... nothing to write home about! Over time, however, you will be the guy smiling at the same Xmas party because you can live off dividends and you won't need to cash in your capitals. All right... I lied to you... **THAT IS SEXY!**

The Power of Dividend Growth: How 3% Turns into 9% and More!

"It is better to have permanent income than to be fascinating."

-Oscar Wilde

Many investors ignore dividend yield as they can't figure how a small 2.50% or 3% can make a real change in their portfolio. Even worse than that, once you have factored inflation (should be calculated at 2.25%), you don't have much left out of this dividend payout! This is why many investors turn their back to dividend stocks and look for the next Google... and lose tons of money in the process!

The true power of dividend investing is not within that poor 3% return that is barely protecting your investment from inflation. The true power, rather, of dividend investing lies within dividend growth. Before we start chasing dividend increases like there's no tomorrow, let's go back to the original concept:

Why Companies Look Forward to Sending You Bigger Dividend Checks

I have few remaining memories of my grandfather. He passed away when I was only 8. I do, however, remember him showing me a nice piece of high quality paper. It was nothing close to any old drab bank statement, this one was different. It had drawings and colors all around it. Just by touching it, you could feel it was an "important piece of paper." On this "work of art" was written "20 shares of Enterprises Bell Canada (now known as BCE). I was fascinated by this piece of paper and when I asked him what it was he simply smiled and then answered: *"This is how you can receive a gift at your birthday each year."* This was my first contact with the concept of dividend payouts.

Dividend investors used to own tangible share certificates of their companies. Each quarter, those investors received dividend checks which they could cash at their bank. Year after year, the checks would get bigger and bigger while the number of shares on the certificate would not be growing. Companies issuing dividends often make the decision to increase their payouts over time. In these days, the principle of dividend payouts and dividend increases work exactly as they used to... but you now receive your electronic deposit in your brokerage account. Nope, nothing sexy about it anymore...

But why in the hell would a company run after you to give you more money? Why on Earth would a company gladly share with you a growing part of their profit? Doesn't the CEO want a better pay check instead? You bet he does, but...

#1 - Companies raise dividends to keep-up with their current dividend yield

The most frequent reason why companies raise their dividend is because their stock went up in value and they want to keep their dividend yield.

For example, if stock A is worth $10 and gives a 5% dividend, the dividend payout is $0.50 per share. But if the stock jumps to $20 over time based on growth and the company doesn't adjust its dividend payout, the same $0.50 will now give a 2.5% dividend. The company will most likely hike its dividend to $1 per share in order to keep the same dividend yield (5%).

Companies usually raise their dividend because they are making more money and therefore the stock value is rising. So it makes sense to reward investors by sharing the same percentage of a bigger profit. The new investors will buy stock A at $20 and earn 5% dividend yield, while the older investor will now own a stock that pays 10% dividend yield ($1 on the original purchase price; $10).

#2 Companies want to keep shareholders on board

Several shareholders own dividend stocks for their... dividend! This is why companies keep increasing their dividend payouts over time, they want to keep their shareholders happy. If they were to leave the payout as is, the dividend would become less interesting over time and many investors might be tempted to sell their stocks and move to a more appealing dividend payer. If investors leave the boat, shares will sink with the sailors...

A dividend that doesn't increase implies several bad signs:

➢ *The company is not growing fast enough;*
➢ *The company is not generating a growing cash flow;*
➢ *The company requires all its cash for its business (this could be good news if they are in an expansion stage but it is not good if they are operating in a grown market);*
➢ *The investor's capital may be eroded by inflation!*

#3 Financial theory applied

According to one financial theory, a company that can't find enough valuable projects and has a cash surplus in its account **will pay a dividend to its shareholders**. The company should do so if its managers think they don't have any other valuable projects on the table. Instead of wasting their money on less profitable ventures or leaving it in a money market fund, the company is encouraged to distribute this excess to the shareholders so they can invest elsewhere.

If a company sees its profits growing but doesn't have any interesting projects on the table; it will likely share the wealth with its investors. This is how companies can grow their dividend payouts year after year provided that their profits follow the same trend.

Examples of Dividend Growth

How does dividend growth theory translate into the real world? I'll share with you 2 examples of dividend growth over time. For each stock, I've selected their price and dividend payout as January 4th 2002 and compared them to data as of September 2011. The goal is to show you how much you would be earning from your initial investment if you were patient enough to wait 9 years with the same stock.

Example #1: National Bank of Canada (NA)

It's not very surprising to use a Canadian bank for a dividend example, but you will surely understand where I'm coming from with such an example. If you look at the graph, you see the stock evolution along with its dividend payout through time:

NA (TSE) – National Bank of Canada

✓ Original price: $29.53

✓ Original dividend payout: $0.96

✓ Original dividend yield: 3.25%

✓ Current dividend payout: $2.84

✓ Current dividend yield (assuming you kept the stock at the original price): **9.61%**

✓ Stock return during that period (dividend excluded): **155.93%**

Okay, I've cheated a little bit by taking a Canadian bank. We all know that they have been rockin' for the past decade. Let's take another stock in another industry. Here's the graph of Telus (T):

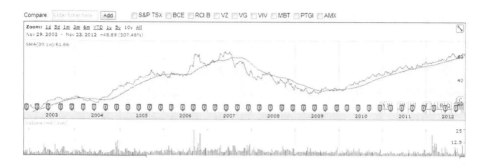

Example #2: Telus Corporation (T)

✓ Original price: $23.55

✓ Original dividend payout: $0.60

✓ Original dividend yield: 2.54%

✓ Current dividend payout: $2.20

✓ Current dividend yield (assuming you kept the stock at the original price): **9.34%**

✓ Stock return during that period (dividend excluded): **155.00%**

As you can see, both stocks used to pay a modest dividend (between 2.50% and 3.50%) and they are both redistributing over 9% in dividends to their most loyal investors. This means that if you invested $100,000 in these 2 stocks in 2002, you would now be earning over $9,000 in dividends per year on top of seeing an investment account worth about $155,000.

If you have more than 10 years in front of you to build your portfolio, I think that I just proved how you can receive the biggest dividend checks you have ever dreamt about!

How to Find Leprechaun's Hidden Gold (and Avoid its Wrath)

With the past 2 examples, I think we are all on the same page. The problem is that looking backward with graphs is pretty easy. All you need is a good hour of your time to waste on Google finance and you can pull out all kinds of crazy graphs showing how it **was** easy to invest money 10 years ago and make a killing.

Back to reality here: each stock you buy won't turn out into a gold producing machine sending you a 9%-10% dividend yield! In fact, even with dividend investing, you will make mistakes and you will end up buying stocks that will eventually have bad financial results that will cut their dividend or worse, suspend it! Any Yellow Page Media (YLO) shareholders in the room? With a diligent (and boring) investing strategy, you will be able to find the hidden pot of gold without allowing the leprechaun to hunt you down.

Key Dividend Growth Ratios and How to Read Them

The first thing you will need when you look at your next purchase is numbers. I think it's the easiest way to build your portfolio: you start with filtering the right stocks through a bunch of numbers. Unfortunately, it's not that easy for Canadians as most free stock filters won't give you all the information you need. Instead of blindly stating key ratios, I'll show you how to do your search with free Canadian stock screeners. Before we get into that, first you need to know what you're looking for, right?

Dividend Yield > 3%

Since you want to build a dividend stock portfolio, the very first thing you should be looking to is the dividend yield. I don't like dividend stocks with a yield under 3%.... unless I know that a company is about to undertake a very aggressive dividend increase policy. I will, however, usually consider lower dividend yield stocks from US companies as they will count as the "secure" section of my portfolio.

For example, I hold Coca-Cola (KO) with a dividend yield at 2.78%. Since KO is diversified and sitting on tons of cash, I consider this stock more like a bond than a stock. On top of that, KO shows the historical habit of doubling its dividend payouts every 6.5 years. Let's return to the concept of 3%+ dividend yield Canadian stocks!

There are over 100 stocks paying more than a 3% dividend yield in Canada, so don't you think that's enough for you to start your search? This is why I usually ignore lower yield stocks for my Canadian assets. On top of that, receiving a 2% dividend is like getting paid a few loonies for shovelling snow out of your driveway; it just doesn't cut it!

5 Year Dividend Growth > 1%

Some people may argue that I'm being generous by allowing some companies with a 1% dividend growth over the past 5 years into my searches. The thing is that we all went through 2008 and several companies had to suspend their dividend increases for at least 2 years. Even Canadian banks put their dividends on hold while they were cashing astronomic profits. That's why I'm giving some of these stocks a break by looking only for companies that were able to increase their dividend over the past 5 years. For the record, when I played with the TMX stock screener, I went from 22 to 13 stocks just by changing the 5 years dividend growth from > 1% to > 5%. In my opinion, 13 stocks is definitely not enough to build a solid portfolio.

Return on Equity (ROE) > 10%

Another important consideration is the ROE. In fact, the ROE is very important. It relates to the ability of a company to generate profits from the investors' money.

Return on Equity = Net Income/Shareholder's Equity

I'm looking for companies able to generate over 10% on shareholder's equity. This shows that the company is able to successfully manage the money invested and that it has a solid plan for growth.

5 Year Annual Income Growth Rate > 1%

We are all looking for growth. That's why I want a company that is able to grow its income over time. Since 2008 is getting in our way, I'm looking for companies that were able to grow by at least 1% their annual income over the past 5 years. If you want your stock to increase its dividend over time, you want to pick companies with income growth.

Current Price / Earnings Ratio < 20

Historically, the S&P TSX (Canadian Index) has been traded around 15 to 16 P/E ratio. If you are able to pick lower P/E ratio stocks than the average, chances are that they are undervalued and that both their stock and dividend will soar in the coming years.

There is one more thing to consider when you look at the P/E ratio: you need to compare it to the company's industry. For example, Canadian Banks P/E ratio sector has always been under 15, so it's not a big surprise to find the big 6 in this category if you run only this filter in your stock screener. On the one hand, Canadian Banks are definitely good investments, but at the same time, don't buy them in the hope of seeing their stocks going back up to a P/E ratio of 15.

Dividend Payout Ratio < 75%

If you are looking for dividend growth stocks, the dividend payout ratio must be one of the very first things you look at. Why is it listed as the last ratio of this section? Simply because you won't be able to find it through a free stock screener! I know, life sucks sometimes! Therefore, you will have to calculate it on your own.

This ratio is very important as it tells you how the company will pay its dividend. If the ratio is close to 100%, that means the company will have to eventually consider financing its dividend (through debts, more equity or selling assets)--which is pretty bad in all cases. The other catastrophic scenario would be a dividend cut. That's why you want to stay away (as much as possible) from a high dividend payout ratio. If the company is at a growth stage, you can extend yourself up to 75%-80%... however, the best case scenario would be to pick stocks under 60%.

The Dividend payout ratio is not that complicated to calculate if you follow this simple formula:

Dividend Payout Ratio = Dividends per Share / Earnings per Share

However, it's **Not that simple**

There are many different characteristics that make the calculation of this ratio much trickier than you would initially think. We decided to take a few, and hopefully this will help you better understand the numbers and how to interpret differences between data sources for the payout ratio.

Leading or trailing dividends?

If you have a dividend portfolio, you hopefully hold a majority of stocks that are raising their dividends in a consistent way. The question would become, what number would you use in formulating whether a company will raise its dividends? For example, suppose we are at 2010-Q4 and here are your best estimates for 2011.

Quarter	Dividend Per Share
2010-Q1	$0.20
2010-Q2	$0.22
2010-Q3	$0.22
2010-Q4	$0.24
2011E-Q1	$0.24
2011E-Q2	$0.26
2011E-Q3	$0.26
2011E-Q4	$0.28

Would you use a dividend per share of:

$0.88 (realized dividends last year)
$0.96 (last dividend annualized)
$1.04 (actual dividend expected in 2011)

You could make a case for all 3 and I can tell you that there is no "right" answer. Some use each one of those numbers and, as you can imagine, it can make a big difference. I use the last dividend annualized as I should have picked a dividend growth stock with no expectation to cut on dividend. On the other hand, playing with "expected dividend" may lead you toward the right direction, since we don't have a crystal ball. The current number (last dividend annualized) is probably the most secure and is therefore the best data to use.

Leading or trailing earnings?

The same situation occurs for earnings, but the effect can be even more dramatic. Why? Earnings tend to fluctuate and one "fluke" quarter with a big loss or a big gain can make a world of difference. In our case, here are the earnings:

Quarter	Earnings Per Share
2010-Q1	$0.68
2010-Q2	$0.75
2010-Q3	-$2.24
2010-Q4	$0.82
2011E-Q1	$0.82
2011E-Q2	$0.88
2011E-Q3	$1.33
2011E-Q4	$0.95

Would you use an earnings per share of:

$0 (realized last year)
$3.26 (last dividend annualized)
$3.98 (actual dividend expected in 2011)

This one is more difficult to judge, but I would say that you tend to take out "extraordinary events" and use a number that is as representative as possible of what can be expected in the future.

Special dividends?

Many companies occasionally pay out special dividends for various reasons. These are certainly nice to have but it's difficult to "assume" they will be paid out in the future, and counting them in the payout ratio or any other dividend statistic can be a difficult decision. For some companies, the "special dividends" are a big part of their payout every year, especially in funds that give out most of their earnings. They will pay a conservative dividend for the first part of the year and then pay out excess earnings at year's end.

Errors

Researching this type of financial data as well as manipulation to include or exclude special factors certainly also opens the possibility for human error. With all of our analysis we do our best to double check everything, but we are always more than happy to look into specific numbers; you can simply contact us.

Debt/Equity Ratio

It's important to consider dividend metrics and sales growth, but there is another important point to consider: the company's balance sheet! You want to make sure the balance sheet is clean so the company can continue to pay dividends over time. A large amount of debt will eventually add pressure on liquidity and therefore affect the dividend growth perspective.

I've chosen the debt/equity ratio as it gives you a clear idea of how the company finances its activities. Each company has the choice of raising debts or shares to finance its projects. The debt/equity ratio is calculated as follows:

Total Liabilities / Shareholders Equity

I'm not including this ratio in my stock screener (see following section) as I think that this ratio needs to be used after you have picked your stock to be put on your radar's list. Depending on the industry and the interest rate wherein the company is evolving, having more or less debt could be an advantage.

For example, interest rates are pretty low at the moment. If a company was able to secure an important debt at a low fixed rate for the next 10 years, it would secure its financial structure to its advantage for several years. This is why it is important to carefully look at the company's vision on financing before looking at this ratio.

How To Use the TMX Stock Screener

To be honest, you don't have many choices when it comes to using a free Canadian stock screener. Among the most popular and useful, you will find the TMX Stock Screener:

http://tmx.quotemedia.com/screener.php?qm_page=88662

and the GlobeInvestor Stock Screener (powered by The Globe & Mail):

http://www.globeinvestor.com/v5/content/filters.html

For the purpose of this book, I've decided to demonstrate how to look through the TMX Stock Screener. I use it for 3 reasons:

#1 You have the ability to add several filters;

#2 You can go back to your original search and modify 1 or more filters and see the new results;

#3 You can edit the column to get as much info as possible in a single snapshot.

Based on the *Key Dividend Ratios* mentioned in the last pages, I've pulled out this screen from the TMX. This section will walk you through each step I used to create "stocks on the radar lists". Keep in mind that this step is useful to create lists and not a portfolio. You will have to look at each stock individually before buying any of them.

Step #1 Get Your Criteria

The first step I take with the TMX is to take off most of their pre-established criteria and change them for my own:

5 Year Annual Income Growth Rate: between 1 and 100 (I want companies that show income growth that could lead to dividend growth).

Current Dividend Yield: over 3% (I want companies that are already paying some healthy dividends and don't want to bother with low dividend paying stocks).

Return on Equity: Over 10% (I want companies that use my money to create wealth. Keep in mind that you'll need to look inside each financial statement to see if the ROE is stable throughout the years).

5 Year Annual Dividend Growth Rate: Over 1% (I'm being more generous as 2008 is creating a big gap in dividend growth stats)

Current Price Earnings Ratio: Under 15 (I want companies that are "undervalued," as they usually represent safer stocks on top of showing a higher potential for growth).

Stock Screener

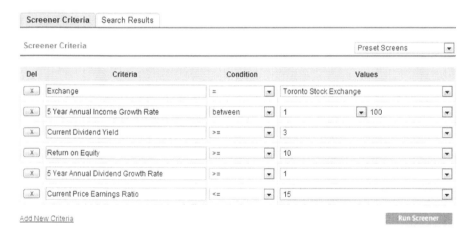

Screener Criteria	Search Results		

Screener Criteria   Preset Screens ▼

Del	Criteria	Condition	Values
X	Exchange	= ▼	Toronto Stock Exchange ▼
X	5 Year Annual Income Growth Rate	between ▼	1 ▼ 100 ▼
X	Current Dividend Yield	>= ▼	3 ▼
X	Return on Equity	>= ▼	10 ▼
X	5 Year Annual Dividend Growth Rate	>= ▼	1 ▼
X	Current Price Earnings Ratio	<= ▼	15 ▼

Add New Criteria   Run Screener

As you can see on this screen, it will take you about 5 minutes to set up your criteria and you will then possess a pretty powerful stock filtering system to start hunting with. If it doesn't provide enough stocks (at the time of writing this book, those filters were giving 11 stocks), you can always go back to this screen and be more "generous".

✓ Changing the dividend yield to 2 instead of 3 will open the doors to stocks with a lower yield, but they can show some growth potential (SNC Lavalin (SNC) for example... besides their problems in Libya!).
✓ Increase the P/E ratio to "under 20" and aim for companies that are "overvalued" as compared to the S&P TSX historic average P/E ratio (around 15 to 16).
✓ If you have more time to look for the reasons behind why the dividend has increased in the past, taking off the 5 yr annual dividend growth rate will definitely give you more choices. *However, you need to be able to find stocks that will start increasing their dividend in the upcoming years and determine reasons why they haven't in the past 5 years.*

Step #2 How to Get Maximum Info in Few Seconds

One of the best features of the TMX is that it allows you to change the information display setting after creating your stock lists. You just click on the "Edit Columns" section as shown on the following page:

Stock Screener

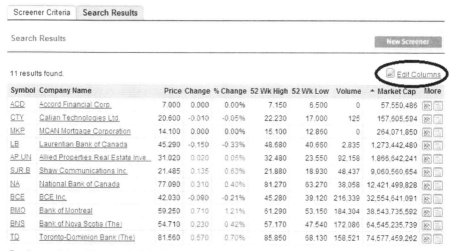

Results generated as of November 23, 2012 10:31 AM EST

You will have the option of showing up to 8 types of data. I don't really like the default settings as I don't care about most "daily stats" such as price, change, volume, etc. Instead, I pull out the following criteria:

➢ Symbol;
➢ Company Name;
➢ Yield instead of "Dividend" (which gives the current dividend yield instead of the dollar amount);
➢ P/E Ratio;
➢ Industry (for asset allocation);
➢ Return on Equity;
➢ 5 Year Annual Revenue Growth;
➢ 5 Year Annual Dividend Growth.

Select up to 10 columns below for the screener results. The Symbol column is always displayed.

☑ Symbol	☑ Company Name	☐ Exchange
☐ Price	☐ Change	☐ % Change
☐ 52 Wk High	☐ 52 Wk Low	☑ Dividend
☐ Volume	☐ Shares Outstanding	☐ Market Cap
☐ 10 Day Avg Volume	☐ 50 Day Moving Avg	☐ 200 Day Moving Avg
☑ P/E Ratio	☐ EPS	☐ More Info (Charts, News)

Profile and Share Information

☐ Sector	☑ Industry	☐ Sub-Industry
☐ # of Employees	☐ 36 Mth Beta	☐ 60 Mth Beta
☐ Shares Floating	☐ Short Interest	☐ Short Interest Ratio
☐ Insider Holdings	☐ Institute Holdings	

Key Ratios

☐ Sales	☐ Current Payout Ratio	☐ Yield
☐ Yield (5 Year Avg)	☑ Return on Equity	☐ Return on Assets
☐ Gross Margin	☐ EBIT Margin	☐ EBITDA Margin
☐ Pre-Tax Profit Margin	☐ Post-Tax Profit Margin	☐ Net Profit Margin
☐ Book Value	☐ Current Ratio	☐ Liquidity Ratio
☐ Leverage Ratio	☐ Quick Ratio	☐ Debt/Common Equity Ratio
☐ Total Debt/Equity Ratio	☐ Price to Revenue Ratio	☐ Price to Equity Ratio
☐ Price to Tangible Book Ratio	☐ Price/Cash Flow Ratio	☐ Price/Free Cash Flow Ratio
☐ Receivables Turnover	☐ Inventory Turnover	☐ Asset Turnover
☐ 3 Yr Annual Revenue Growth	☑ 5 Yr Annual Revenue Growth	☐ 3 Yr Annual Income Growth
☐ 5 Yr Annual Income Growth	☐ 3 Yr Annual Dividend Growth	☑ 5 Yr Annual Dividend Growth

Step #4 Study Your List

Now that you have pulled out all the relevant information, it will be much easier to compare each stock and determine which one should be part of your "radar list". After modifying your columns, you will get a screener providing a lot of key information:

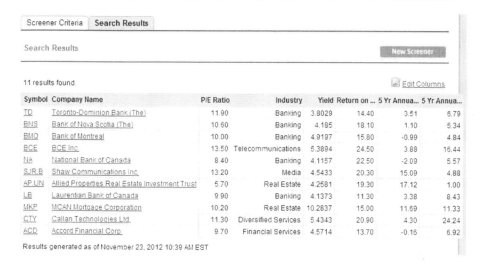

This is a great opportunity to discover "less sexy" stocks such as Allied Properties REIT (AP.UN) or MCAN Mortgage Corp (MKP). Another interesting point is that you can see that not all Canadian banks fit the tougher dividend growth criteria. Chances are, however, that BNS, TD, BMO and NA will show better investment returns than its peers over the next 5 years.

Building Your Way Through Wealth – How To Build Your Portfolio

"I have the simplest tastes. I am always satisfied with the best."

-Oscar Wilde

Now that you had fun playing with your stock screener, it's time to get serious: **how do you build your portfolio?** Do you simply put 20-30 stocks together with a bunch of similar stats and rake in the dividends? You can certainly do it (I know investors that have the 6 banks and just wait for their quarterly dividend), but I think you can do a lot better than that. There is obviously no secret method where you can get the best dividend picks all the time. However, if you follow some of the techniques explained in this book, I'm certain you'll be able to combine both stock appreciation and dividend growth.

The purpose of this section is to provide you with some tools for building your portfolio. These techniques don't contain the absolute truth but they will prevent you from chasing too much yield or too much growth without considering investing fundamentals. This is how I will teach you to build your own quadrants to compare your stocks, use diversification to your advantage and as a bonus, I'll also show you how to cheat on your investing strategy (because dividend investing can get boring sometimes ;-) .

4 Quadrants For a Better Understanding of Your Portfolio

The first thing you should do when you want to build a portfolio is to place stocks that are on your radar into 3 different quadrants. This technique is used to compare each of them and make quick decisions based on your dividend growth investing strategy. What is cool about quadrants is that they are easy to use, easy to understand and don't require much time (I know, I'm lazy sometimes ;-)).

The idea of building a quadrant system is quite simple: first, you select two characteristics you want to compare (consider dividend yield and dividend payout ratio). Next, you compile the data for all your stocks with both characteristics. Once you have all the data, you simply have to position each stock according to their yield (on the X Axis) and their payout ratio (on the Y Axis). Here's a quick example:

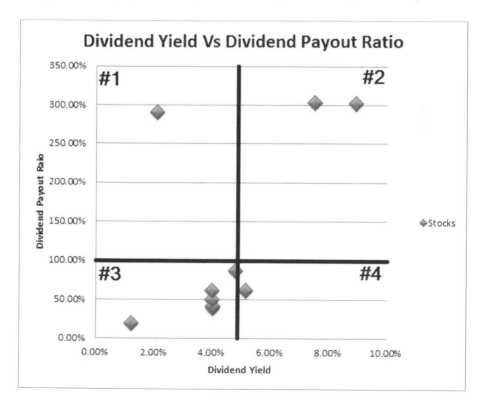

In this example, it is quite obvious that you would like to get as many of your stocks in the #4 quadrant (high dividend yield with low payout ratio). The less attractive quadrant is #1 (low dividend yield with high dividend payout ratio). Within minutes, you can determine which stocks are good additions to your portfolio and which are not.

Quadrants have been used over and over for several purposes. Companies use them to position their products (high end vs., low end, mass consumer vs., niche, etc), we will use them to position your stock. If you hope to live off dividends one day, you need to seek stocks that:

➢ *Provide a healthy dividend at first;*
➢ *Grow their dividend over time;*
➢ *Grow their income over time (so they can keep up with their dividend and provide you with capital growth at the same time).*

In order to find those stocks, you can use the following 3 different quadrants:

Dividend Yield Vs., Dividend Payout Ratio

The first quadrant we will look at is the one comparing the stock's dividend yield to its ability to keep it (the dividend payout ratio). The first thing we look at as dividend investors is obviously the dividend yield. But instead of chasing blindly the yield as a dog running after a cat that just crossed a boulevard, you are better off watching the dividend payout ratio to make sure that you don't see your dividend (or your dog) getting squished!

It's always more fun when you have a true example, so I've pulled out 10 stocks off the TSX 60 to show you how they compare on the quadrant. Here's my data compilation:

Ticker	Dividend Yield	Dividend Payout Ratio
CNQ	1.24%	19.21%
ECA	4.05%	39.36%
NA	4.05%	41.40%
BNS	4.02%	50.01%
POW	5.18%	61.32%
T	4.01%	62.02%
HSE	4.82%	86.96%
WN	2.12%	289.98%
ERF	8.92%	302.00%
PWT	7.53%	303.00%

As you can see, you have some pretty high and pretty low dividend yields and payout ratios. That doesn't mean, however, that all the low yields have a low payout ratio and vice-versa. This is what the quadrant will show you in a heartbeat:

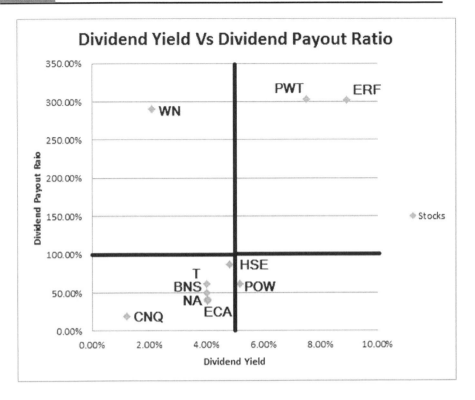

From this perspective, the less attractive quadrant for me is the one over the 100% line. I don't really mind if the dividend yield is high or not at this point, because if they give more that they can then they'll eventually have to cut on their dividend or sell assets to keep the miracle going.

In an ideal world, we would only pick stocks in the #4 quadrant as those stocks should provide high & sustainable dividend yield. Unfortunately, we only have one stock that fits in this category and it is Power Corp (POW). However, you also have some healthy dividend payers with decent payout ratio (T, BNS, NA & ECA). CNQ is not offering an interesting yield even though the company would be able to pay the distribution forever with such low payout ratio. As for HSE, it's pretty close to not making the cut because of its high payout ratio but it should still provide some great dividends. I would need more time to analyze this one to see if I want this stock in my portfolio, but it would not be my first pick either.

Dividend Yield Vs Dividend Growth

Once you have found companies that have sustainable dividend levels, the second thing you want to look at is how their dividend yield compares to their dividend growth. A company dividend yield could be high because it has been devalued for specific reasons or because the stock is following a bigger trend (as it is the case in a bear market for example). However, if you can find high dividend yield payers with low payout ratios **and** showing 5 year dividend growth; you are getting closer to a great dividend pick!

By comparing dividend yield and dividend growth over 5 years, you want to pick the highest yield with the highest dividend growth. Continuing the same example, here are my data for the following quadrant:

Ticker	Dividend Yield	5 Yr Dividend Growth
CNQ	1.24%	20.78%
ECA	4.05%	19.82%
NA	4.05%	6.32%
BNS	4.02%	7.93%
POW	5.18%	8.97%
T	4.01%	12.78%
HSE	4.82%	14.66%
WN	2.12%	15.75%
ERF	8.92%	-18.00%

You can already guess that ERF will be out of my stock picks ;-). Please also note that I had to take Penn West (PWT) out of the following quadrant as 5 years of data wasn't available as it was previously an income trust. Here's the quadrant:

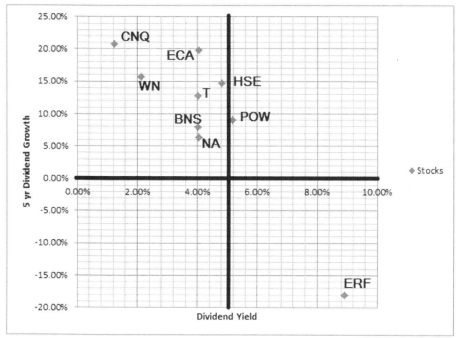

This time, the most interesting quadrant is #2 as it would provide stocks with high dividend yield and high dividend growth. Then again, we have POW sitting alone as an example in this category. However, we have HSE, ECA, T, BNS and NA (in this order) that are interesting. They all show an interesting dividend yield (more than 4%) while providing great dividend growth.

Another thing that needs to be highlighted is the ability of CNQ to increase its dividend significantly. Even if the dividend yield is minimal, it should catch your attention to see what happened with this stock and its dividend over time. For example, a quick search would have taught you that CNQ doubled its dividend in the past 5 years and also went from $0.05 to $0.36 dividend per share in the past 10 years. While the dividend yield is not really impressive today, the stock jumped by almost 1000% in 10 years. This is certainly something to think of before making your final decisions!

5 Years Dividend Growth Vs 5 Years Revenue Growth

After doing those 2 quadrants, you definitely positioned your stocks in terms of which ones have the most attractive dividend yield and dividend growth. The next 2 quadrants will take a different look at the same stocks; we will see if those companies can sustain their level of dividend over time.

Why compare the 5 years dividend growth with the 5 years revenue growth? Because the first one depends on the latter. Since dividends are paid with after tax income, you want to make sure the company has enough fund to keep its dividend payouts. More importantly, it will tell you more about the dividend distribution strategy of the company.

A low dividend growth combined with a high revenue growth (quadrant #1) demonstrates that the company is in a growing stage. The company believes it is best to use its cash flow to push the company to another level instead of giving back to the shareholders. This is good to increase your chances of seeing a capital gain, but it's another thing if you are looking for dividend growth. If you are at the early stage of your portfolio (e.g. you don't intend to withdraw money right away), those are the stocks that will add more punch to your portfolio while providing you with a nice dividend at a same time.

On the other hand, a high dividend growth with negative revenue growth (quadrant #4) demonstrates that the company is throwing sands in your eyes so you don't see what goes wrong and suffice yourself with a great dividend. In this situation, the company dividend payout ratio will probably increase over time, which is not a good sign for an investor.

The perfect scenario would be to find a company with a steady dividend growth and revenue growth at a similar level. This tells you that the company is growing and has the intention of giving money back to its shareholders at the same time. Following my example, here are the data from my stock list:

Ticker	5 Yr Dividend Growth	5 Yr Revenue Growth
CNQ	20.78%	6.47%
ECA	19.82%	-14.63%
NA	6.32%	-3.95%
BNS	7.93%	3.40%
POW	8.97%	0.38%
T	12.78%	5.96%
HSE	14.66%	8.90%
WN	15.75%	-0.13%
ERF	-18.00%	-7.35%
PWT	N/A	N/A

Before using the quadrant, you can always see that CNQ, BNS, T and HSE are following an interesting trend on both revenue and dividend growth. Now let's take a look at the big picture:

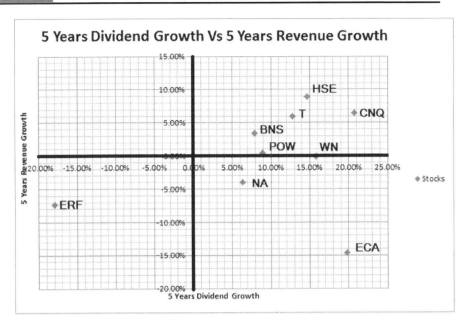

See how things get clear on a great graph? We are lucky with our picks as most of them are in the quadrant #2, which means positive dividend growth with positive revenue growth. On this graph, the more healthy stocks in term of dividend payout strategy are CNQ, HSE, T and BNS. I would throw ERF and ECA in the garbage in a heartbeat, but I would take a look at National Bank (NA) closely. Why? Because Canadian banks had it rough in 2008 and that might have temporarily affected their revenue growth. If you look at NA financial statements, you will notice that in 2008 and 2009, they had to take a special loss on Asset Backed Commercial Papers (ABCP) which they were the biggest supplier in Canada (and we all know what happened to all those credit default swaps and other complicated commercial papers…). Since then, they show a healthy revenue growth while maintaining a decent payout ratio. This is another great example of why you can't base your decision on a single quadrant!

P/E Ratio Vs 5 Year Income Growth

The last quadrant (but not the least) is comparing the P/E ratio with the 5 year income growth. It's like comparing future assumptions with past results. The P/E ratio is the current evaluation of a stock by the market. A high P/E ratio means that the market is anticipating an important growth. You will most likely find stocks that may be overrated in this category (just think of RIM a few years ago). P/E ratio starts to get high when they are over the bar of 20. The historical P/E Ratio of the TSX is 16. Anything over 20 means that you expect very high income later on.

On the other side, if you have a low P/E ratio, it is probably because the stock is evolving in a mature industry... or that the stock is undervalued. It is obviously tricky to determine which stocks are price correctly or not. Keep in mind that the P/E ratio will be greatly affected by the stock market's assumptions. For example, after 2 years of deceiving financial results, RIM has traded at a P/E ratio as low as 3.81! This doesn't mean that the company is undervalued; it means that the market doesn't see how the company can keep up with its previous results!

This quadrant will help you find stocks with the lowest P/E ratio possible, but the highest income growth at the same time.

Ticker	P/E Ratio	5 Yr Income Growth
CNQ	29.3	-9.43%
ECA	19.8	-27.31%
NA	10.4	7.93%
BNS	10.9	4.71%
POW	11.9	-5.57%
T	15.9	4.81%
HSE	12	-15.37%
WN	18.2	21.57%
ERF	14.9	-8.59%
PWT	13.5	N/A

Look at stocks in the quadrant #1 (low P/E ratio with positive income growth). Those stocks are more likely evolving in a stable environment (this is why their P/E ratio is lower) but with income growth (they are able to increase their income in a mature or saturated industry). Those types of companies will likely only become stronger over time:

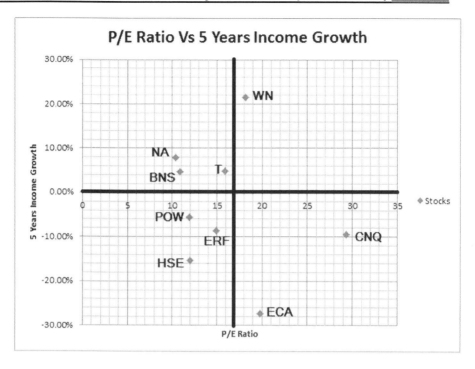

This quadrant shows interest in 3 stocks: NA, BNS, T. As I just mentioned that it is important to look at the financial statement, NA shows strong income growth while negative revenue growth. The answer lies in the ABCP losses. BNS and Telus are 2 other great stocks showing lower P/E ratio with positive income growth. These 3 stocks are evolving in mature industries where massive growth is not expected. As a dividend growth investor, you should be looking for more stability than rollercoaster growth anyway!

Cross Referencing the Quadrants

Now that you know how to use the 4 quadrants, the most important thing is yet to come: **use all 4 of them!** Don't get complaisant and use 1 or 2 comparative measures. Use all 4 of them and ask yourself a few questions, as I just did. Don't jump to a conclusion and don't be afraid to look into financial statements once in a while to understand how a stock is less attractive in one quadrant compared to the others.

By cross referencing the 4 quadrants, you will find stocks that are coming back more regularly (in this example, we have Scotia Bank (BNS) and Telus (T) that fit in the right quadrants all the time. In my opinion, those 2 stocks should be part of my portfolio (and they are at the moment of writing this book!) since they meet most of my criteria.

Then, you have National Bank (NA), Husky Energy (HSE), Power Corp. (POW) that are interesting but with some flaws (sometimes, they couldn't qualify under the right quadrant). If you can explain those flaws by contextual events (2008 credit crash, oil price variation), you may want to add them to your portfolio or, at least, add them to your radar list.

Then, you have the other stocks that didn't qualify half of the time (ECA, WN and CNQ). I would not be tempted to add them to my portfolio as they miss the target on a few important metrics. It doesn't mean that they are not interesting at all, but in a vision of dividend growth, I would have skipped them since I can find better purchases.

Finally, you have more "obvious" rejects: PWT and ERF with definite problems. Ridiculously high dividend payouts mixed with decreasing income show nothing good right now. Do you really want to throw your money out of the window?

So out of 10 stocks and 4 quadrants, you have:

- ✓ 2 obvious picks (BNS & T)
- ✓ 3 interesting picks (NA, HSE, POW)
- ✓ 3 not very good picks (ECA, WN and CNQ)
- ✓ 2 "throw in the garbage" picks (PWT & ERF)

Doing this exercise can require some times as you first need to put all your stocks in an excel spread sheet, find all the metrics and create your quadrant. In order to do it, here's a very easy tutorial for excel users:

- ✓ #1 Create a table as shown in this book (ticker, metric1, metric2)
- ✓ #2 Select data only in metric #1 and metric #2 (the 2 columns)
- ✓ #3 Click on "insert", then "other charts" and select "X Y (Scatter)"

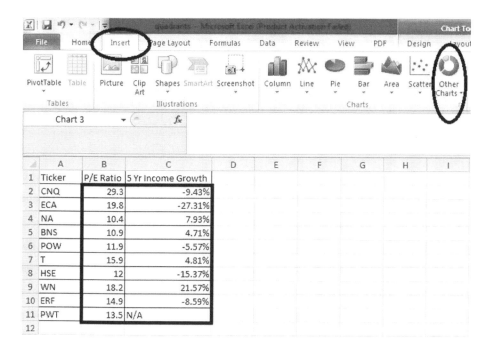

- ✓ #4 You'll get your points in a graph. You select Chart Layouts and take the circled one in the second line of options:

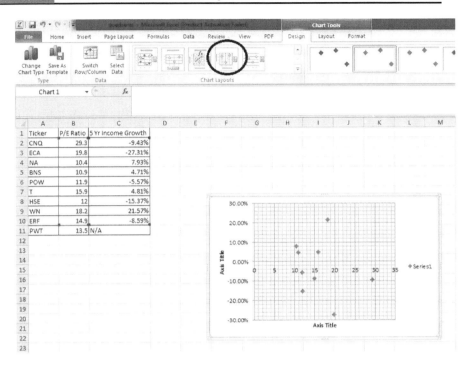

✓ #5 Then, you simply have to print it and add the stock name besides each dot and you have your quadrant!

Diversification is the Key For Successful Investors

Playing with screeners and quadrants is a lot of fun indeed, and those 2 parts of the book will definitely help you build a strong "stocks on the radar" list. But what if you have 20 or 30 of them and you only have $10,000 to invest? And worse, what if you have 5 or 10 stocks from the same industry? Since you can't buy all the stocks that fit your criteria, you need to find ways to select the right ones among your list....hint: this is the part where dividend investing becomes less sexy as we are reducing the risk of your portfolio ;-)

The best criteria to make such decisions are to consider the diversification of your portfolio. I'm sure you have heard the term "diversification" a thousand time and you are probably sick or hearing about it or asset allocation. But if there is one thing you need to remember it's that you won't get very far with your portfolio if you are not well diversified! There are several ways to diversify your portfolio, and we will look at all of them in a minute...

Diversification by sector

Among all types of diversification, sector investing is my favourite. After looking at how the market reacts over financial news, I noticed that there are more emotional than rational factors influencing the value of a stock! When the market is enticed by a sector, chances are that most stocks in this sector will benefit from a push. Sometimes this push is totally justifiable, and some other times, it's completely ridiculous. The best example was the massive value drop of any Canadian bank in 2008. Investors put all banks from all countries in the same basket. This is how Canadian banks lost more than 50% of their stock value in 4 months:

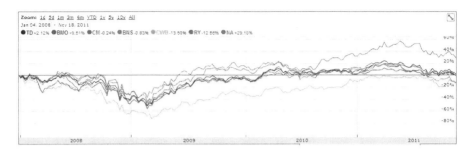

This was obviously unjustified. This also shows why you should not put buy all the stocks from the same industry. If the market was right in 2008, you would have lost 50% of your portfolio for a very long time (anybody get caught in the Canadian techno bubble in 1999-2000?).

The Canadian stock market shows a lot of great dividend stocks in some sectors. For example, you won't have a hard time finding what you are looking for within financials, telecoms or energy. While I just showed you how your portfolio could fluctuate in a short period of time if you have invested in the financials, the energy sector is no different. The reason why you don't want to concentrate too much in a specific sector is that you can't know for sure if it's a good move or not. You think you are smarter and that you can't pick wrong? Well that's only true if you are already a multimillionaire trader and have made your money through stock trading. You're not? Then you are not smarter than me or the average investor. Just stick with a good sector diversification instead of playing casino ;-).

I believe that investing solely in Canada would greatly restrain your portfolio as 50% of the stock market is in the financial or energy sectors. It's therefore pretty hard to identify strong dividend payers in each industry when you're limiting your research to Canadian stocks. Adding a US portion to your investment will definitely boost your dividend growth perspective and your overall portfolio yield. This leads us to the next type of diversification:

Diversification by geography

With a strong Canadian dollar, an undervalued U.S. stock market and an incredibly diversified economy, you would be a fool to ignore the US market and concentrate on Canadian stocks only. I understand that you might be afraid of the currency risks or the tax implication, and that's why we will cover both aspects later on in this book.

U.S. stocks provide you with a unique advantage you can rarely find in the Canadian markets: an indirect access to emerging markets growth! What do Procter & Gamble (PG), McDonal's (MCD), Johnson & Johnson (JNJ), Colgate Palmolive (CL), Coca-Cola (KO), PepsiCo (PEP), and Yum Brand (YUM) have in common? They are all solid companies, great dividend payers and show important presence in the emerging markets. There are literally tons of US companies with solid balance sheets exploring the emerging market and using their cash flow and experience to develop those markets. What's the favourite Chinese junk food? It's PFK (YUM) and McDonald's (MCD). What do they drink? Most likely Coke (KO). Which toothpaste will they I use in a few years? You guessed it... Colgate!

Some of those companies are not only diversified geographically, but also within their product & services offering. Johnson & Johnson has so many different products that they are as diversified as a mutual fund by itself! You don't find those types of companies in Canada and this is why you need to add some Dividend aristocrats or Dividend Champions to your "buy list". For my own personal portfolio (read: this is not advice), I prefer to buy strong companies established in several countries with several products such as JNJ & KO instead of buying bonds. They are the part of my portfolio that I consider "low risk". They pay more than government bonds and they are also providing some capital appreciation potential on top of it!

Why go U.S. instead of going with Europe or Emerging markets? Simply because it's darn easy to trade United States stocks (all you need is a brokerage account). Also, our dollar is almost at parity with the U.S. dollar. Accordingly, it won't affect much of your portfolio and you will have an amazing window to pick amongst the most profitable, diversified and stable companies around the world.

Also, depending on the timing of the market, the U.S. stock markets can be more attractive than the Canadian market. For example, in 2009, the stock rally was more impressive on the Canadian side for the first 9 months. After this period, investors should have considered U.S. stocks as they hadn't followed the Canadian crazy pace while some companies where showing great results. This is how the U.S. stock market did better than the Canadian market in 2010... Instead of trying to guess which stock market is best, you are better off playing on both sides of the border instead ;-).

You don't need to have 100K to consider investing in the U.S. market. I offer portfolio models toward the end of this book with U.S. investment for a $10,000 portfolio. The key is to have RRSP room due to tax implication. Keep reading and you'll know why!

Diversification by size

You can also diversify your portfolio according to market capitalization. Generally, large market capitalization stocks are less likely to suffer from high fluctuations since they are very big companies. On the other hand, small caps are seen as growing companies that can be more affected by the economy. In a bullish environment, the small caps are the big winners.

However, with the "post 2008" stock markets, any stock can suffer from high fluctuation. When the TSX drops by 3% in a single day, most stocks are hit. On top of that, small caps usually don't pay dividends. Therefore, if you ask me if I care about market capitalization when I pick a stock, I'll tell you *"hell, no!"*. But that's just me ;-).

How to Quickly Manage Your Diversification

One of the most important reasons why you should have bought this book is because you don't have enough time to properly manage an active portfolio. Dividend investing can be appealing as it doesn't require you to check your portfolio every week. The trick is that you still need to manage your portfolio once it is built and make sure that you are not over- exposing your investments to specific risks.

In order to do so, I would suggest you use 2 methods to ensure that you don't spend too much time on diversification so you don't put yourself at risk.

a) Make a sector distribution list

The first thing to do before building your portfolio is to identify the sector that you want to invest in. I've showed you how to determine great stocks regardless of their industry, now you will do the opposite: you will look at all the sectors and then select the one you want in your portfolio. Then, you will be able to go back to your stock on the radar list and pick the one that fit your sector needs.

Think of selecting sectors that should do well in the future and pick strong dividend payers in each of them. This way, although you might be wrong on the sector, you will own the "best" stocks in each industry. Concentrating on one sector (such as energy, financials or telecoms) will create greater fluctuations in your portfolio. Depending on what you are looking for (growth, steady income, etc.), you may classify your sector like this. Growth sectors will offer greater capital gain potential but you will have to be ready to ride higher fluctuation as well. Steady income sectors will provide a nice steady dividend but might not be part of your sexiest investment.

Here's a quick review of each Canadian sector (I used sectors description from TMX stock screener to make your life easier if you filter per sector).

Basic Materials: Canada has been known for its resources since its discovery back in 1492! We have a lot of basic materials and a lot of companies listed on our stock market. Most importantly, this includes the Energy sub sector. If you look at the highest dividend payer in this sector, you will find several oil & gas related stocks. I think that this is a sector that will outperform over the next 10 years as the world is looking for more and more resources. However, it will also include a great deal of fluctuation upon recessions or sovereign debts concerns (as the Eurozone faced back in 2010 & 2011). It's definitely a sector where you can find great dividend growth stocks, but you will also find more growth than dividends ;-).

Conglomerate & Consumer Goods: Remember how I was telling you that you'll miss something when you focus solely on Canadian dividend stocks to build your portfolio? You have a great example with conglomerates & consumer goods sector. The first sector offers 1 stock paying over 3% dividend yield, the latter offers only 17 stocks. Since you have the opportunity to pick amazing U.S. companies, I would not be tempted to select Canadian stocks in this category. In general, consumer goods are separated in cyclical and non-cyclical depending if the company follows the economic cycle or not. Cyclical stocks are good when you are in expansion, while non-cyclical companies make great defensive stocks.

Financials: Obviously one of the richest pools of Canadian stocks. Canada's banking system has been the pride of the country since 2008. Companies in this sector are evolving in mature and secure markets. This is how you can benefit from a great combination of both growth and dividend growth. Don't expect to make double digits returns but you will definitely be close to it if you add both capital gains and dividend yield at the end of the year. In addition to banks, insurance companies and investment firms, the TMX stock screener also includes Real Estate Income Trusts (REITs) in this category. Since I think it's a whole different beast, I'll cover REITs separately in this book with a complete chapter on them. Let's just say for now that REITs will bring you a lot of income stability, but don't expect much capital growth from them over a long term investment horizon.

Healthcare: Once again, the Canadian healthcare industry is not big enough to include world class dividend payers. You can count only 6 stocks paying over 3% dividend yield as of November 2011. I don't appreciate healthcare stocks in a dividend growth perspective as even the U.S. pharmaceuticals will always be dependent on future R&D discoveries, which incur a consistent level of high expenses. This is why I'm not all that interested in this sector, especially on the Canadian perspective.

Industrial goods: You will only find a few companies in this sector, but it might be worth it to take a look at the 12 stocks paying over 3% in dividend. I would be tempted to pick one stock in this sector as it follows the economy, but on a slower pace as they deal with companies.

Services: This is another great Canadian sector, as I was able to pull 68 stocks while I was writing this book. The services sector needs to be broken down into sub-sectors such as:

➤ *Retail (Reitmans, Le Château, Indigo, Leon;*
➤ *Media (Astral, Corus, Torstar, Transcontinental);*
➤ *Food & Restaurant (Boston Pizza, A&W, Pizza).*

There are also many other companies that don't fit those "major" sub-sectors such as AutoCanada, Gamehost, Caliant Technologies, Genivar, etc. You will find interesting stocks in this sector and you can definitely pick 4-5 stocks without even touching the same industry twice (I highly doubt that Reiman's sales are in line with Genivar's engineering consulting services). For each industry, you have to ask yourself if it's an expanding (engineering), mature (media) or declining (paper media!) phase.

Technology: To my great surprise, a big part of the technology sector involves a relatively mature market. The big telecoms (Rogers, Bell, Shaw & Telus) are definitely the biggest point of interest in this sector. They are in a similar environment to Canadian banks since they are all big players in a small and well-guarded playground. While we often consider techno stocks as high risk and volatile, mature companies paying dividend will react differently. This is without a doubt a great addition to your portfolio.

As you can see, if you go sector by sector, you'll notice that the Canadian market shows somewhat of a lack of diversification. It is interesting enough to build a solid core portfolio but some additions on the U.S. side will be necessary to limit the volatility of your investment account. In the meantime, there is another way to manage the volatility of your portfolio...

b) Use the Beta

You may or may not be familiar with a stock's beta. If you have taken any financial classes at University, you will have seen it in the Capital Asset Pricing Model (CAPM). So for those who don't know what the beta is, here's a quick explanation.

The beta of a stock is a statistical measure telling you the level of volatility of a stock compared to the stock market as a whole. Say what? In other words, it tells you if your stock will swing more or less than the stock market (on the up and down side). Stock that moves according to the market (so, not more or less volatile) will have a beta of 1. A 1.2 beta will go up 20% more than the market while a 0.80 will move 20% less. If you hold shares of XYZ with a beta of 1.2

and the market goes up by 1% today, your shares will be up 1.20%. This is also true if the market goes down by 1%.

Don't worry, you don't have to calculate the stock's beta as you can get it for free for any stock with Google Finance[10]. While picking up your stocks, you should have most of your stocks with a beta smaller than 1. Why? Because dividend stocks are the best... and they fluctuate less due to the fact that investors appreciate holding them for the dividend!

What you really need to do is to calculate your portfolio beta. This is quite easy to do. All you need is to build a simple excel spread sheet with your stocks, market value, % of your portfolio for each of them (market value of your stock divided by the market value of your portfolio), the beta for each stock and the pro-rated beta (percentage of the stock * the beta) as showed in the following example:

Ticker	Market Value	% of Portfolio	Beta	Pro-rated Beta
HSE	$5,000	14%	0.9	0.12
NA	$4,000	11%	0.5	0.06
BNS	$7,000	20%	0.7	0.15
T	$8,000	23%	0.3	0.06
GH	$6,000	17%	0.8	0.14
CVL	$5,000	14%	0.9	0.13
Total	$35,000	100%		0.65

[10] www.google.com/finance

In this quick example, you have a portfolio with a beta of 0.65. Thx to Telus (T) and National Bank (NA) that contributed to lower the beta. Without these 2 stocks, we would have a beta of 0.82, which would correspond to a more aggressive portfolio.

Depending on what your goals are (long term growth vs., creating a source of income), you should aim for a different beta. More aggressive dividend stocks will show a 0.75 to 1 beta (as they follow the market fluctuation on top of providing a healthy dividend). This is the case for Energy related stocks, for example. More defensive dividend stocks will show a 0.50 to 0.25 beta (as they are much more stable than the stock markets).

If you are retired and concerned about market fluctuation, you should concentrate on stocks with a smaller beta (below 0.60). This will ensure fewer headaches during market crashes while you keep cashing your dividend checks. The opposite (looking for a higher beta close to 1) is also true if you are looking for long term growth doubled with high dividend payouts.

Quick trading hint: When you are about to buy a stock, buy the high beta stocks on your list during bear markets (as they will drop with the stock market) and reserve low beta stocks for bull markets (as their main asset is their dividend and not their ability to capture market growth).

Sometimes You Gotta Cheat

All right, before you go see my Dividend Holdings[11] on The Dividend Guy Blog and you notice that not all my stocks are following the technique described in this book, it's time to be honest with you:

✓ It is VERY important to have a core strategy and respect it. If you have a solid investment process, you will build a solid investment portfolio.
✓ Solid investment processes are useful, effective but boring, so sometimes I cheat and I don't fully obey my investment strategy.

Why am I cheating from time to time? It's quite simple:

✓ I'm young and I have a long term horizon – so I can take higher risks.
✓ I used to be an aggressive trader and succeeded with my previous strategy – so I'm still tempted from time to time.
✓ I like dividend, but I like some heavy growth as well.

What's the morale of this example? It's that maybe you should allow yourself a buffer where you invest in more risky stocks. They can pay dividend or not but they should never represent an important part of your portfolio. It should not derail you from your core investment strategy and you should not have more than 1 stock outside of your strategy. If not, it's like not having an investing strategy at all!

If you just started investing or if you are about to retire and look toward a more conservative portfolio **I don't think that diverting from your investment strategy is a good idea**. Because when you ignore some financial ratios for the sake of growth, you also greatly increase the risk of your portfolio. Make sure that you don't become a gambler and that you instead remain an investor.

---

[11] http://www.thedividendguyblog.com/dividend-stock-holdings/

There is another moment where you have to cheat...

There is also another moment when it's okay to pick a stock that doesn't fulfill all your investing rules; this situation is called "2008".

In my opinion, 2008 is a statistical error. This is a point in the stock market history where most metrics don't make sense. While this wasn't the first (and the last) recession the stock market has faced, it had a great impact on all companies. This is how several great dividend payers (such as Banks) suspended their good old habit of increasing their dividend. You also have the whole energy sector which depends on the price of oil that went through a rough time. Remember, the barrel went down as low as $35 at one point (while most companies projected the price barrel over $100 and needed a price of $75 to be profitable).

2008 should not be the excuse for everything. Far from it. A bad company is a bad company and it has been greatly affected during the latest recession. However, some great companies may not fit your search criteria if you consider 2008 and 2009 data. So if you don't find enough stocks meeting your criteria (or they are all in the same sector), you may want to loosen up your search in order to find hidden gems. This is why it's more important than ever to take a look at why the company couldn't meet all your requirements instead of tossing it away like garbage after an initial search.

I'm not saying that you should find "excuses" for non-performing or under-performing stocks. 'Cause if you dig deeper enough and you are creative; you will find excuses for any stocks crossing your screen. What is really important is to *understand* what happened in 2008-2009 for each stock you are about to select. For example, it is pretty obvious that Husky Energy (HSE) went through a tough period because its business relies on a high price of oil. But if you now think that the barrel should remain over $75 in the coming years, you may want to consider this stock in your portfolio.

Just remember; cheating could be exciting but in most cases, you will end-up with a bad relationship... with your portfolio, obviously ;-)

The Dividend Growth Investor Jedi Code

You should not be impressed by the following section if you have been reading carefully everything I wrote so far in this book. I'm basically doing a huge recap of all the investing rules / Jedi Code you should follow when you build your portfolio.

It is very important to make that recap now as we are going to enter a more advanced section in the next chapter. So if you don't master your investing rules, you won't be able to follow the parade.

Note that you can adapt your investing Jedi Code to your own needs. This is my method to find high quality dividend growth stocks but I'm not your God and you shall not listen to everything I tell you (all the time)... ;-)

The Dividend Growth Investor Jedi Code

1. You shall look for healthy food (dividend >3% + dividend growth >0% over 5 years.
2. You shall prefer steady growth and fast growing success (P/E <15 , ROE >10%);
3. You shall not be greedy (select stocks with low dividend payout ratio >75%);
4. You shall combine your strengths to succeed (use the 4 quadrants);
5. You shall not concentrate too much---open your mind (diversify your portfolio);
6. You shall control your anger (use beta and sector list to control diversification);
7. You shall not cheat, though cheating is not forbidden.

All right! Now you can take off your Jedi tunic and open up your computer. Let's trade baby!

Trading 201: All You Need To Know Before Pulling The Trigger

"Everything popular is wrong."

-Oscar Wilde

It is nice to look carefully at ratios and use your stock filter like a pro. However, this doesn't tell you when it's the right moment to pull the trigger and pick the stock you are secretly coveting. As most people love to buy stocks, you may not find that this is a big problem, but you might be wondering when to sell your stocks and how to manage your whole portfolio.

I'll tell you upfront, I'm not a big fan of market timing in the sense that I don't support investment thesis where you can be in and out the market with your portfolio in order to benefit from the growth period and avoid bear markets.

As a dividend investor, you should be primarily in the stock market **to earn your dividend payout**. This is why I don't think that market timing is a good idea for you. However, it doesn't mean that you can't wait until you have the "best" timing to buy a stock or to get rid of it.

This section of the book has been designed to help you:

✓ Know when it's the right timing to buy a stock;
✓ Know how you can limit your loss or when to sell a stock;
✓ Know how many stocks you should hold to have a solid portfolio;
✓ Know how many trades you should be making in your book each year.

Finding Early Triggers - When To Buy a Stock

The first step you need to do when building your portfolio is to obviously buy some stocks! Is there a magic secret to buy the right stock at the right moment? Man, if I knew that, I would be writing this book from my 60 feet long boat parked in the Bahamas…. But that ain't the case.

However, it doesn't mean that you can't find hints on your entry point. There are a few pointers that will indicate to you when the stock market is offered at discount and that you can benefit from this seasonal sale.

Be ready… aim… fire!

The very first trick to buy the right stock at the right time is obviously to be in a position to do it. Most investors (including myself once in a while) are very impatient. When they run their stock screener and find a few stocks they want to buy, they can't help and pull the trigger right away. If the stock you have found is meeting your requirements, then chances are that you will make a good buy overall. You can, however, make it more profitable by being a little bit more patient.

This is how building liquidity while maintaining a "stocks on the radar" list will help you seize the opportunity you have been waiting for. Here are a few ways you can build your liquidity:

Using a systematic plan: The easiest way to build enough cash is to set an automatic investment into your brokerage account. I suggest you invest at the same time you get your pay check. If you have a bi-weekly deposit, you should be having a bi-weekly investment setup. It doesn't have to be a huge amount. In fact, $50 every 2 weeks can amount to $1,000 in a year in your investment account. This should be enough for you to buy a stock. The more aggressive you are with your budget, the faster you will build a solid investment portfolio.

You can either invest the money in a money market fund (for conservative portfolio) or through an index fund (that replicates the Canadian or U.S. stock market). If you select the latter, you will be participating in the stock market before buying your own stocks which is a great way to start. I personally use the Altamira Canadian Index Fund (NBC814) when I have money to put on the side before my next trade.

Line of credit or RRSP loan (leverage): Unless you know that the money is coming (i.e. you are waiting to get a bonus, a salary adjustment or a tax return), I would not advise that you use leverage to build your dividend portfolio. I'm actually a big fan of leveraging but I should write a whole book about the topic before I feel comfortable telling you it's a good way to invest in your situation. However, having a line of credit ready to provide enough liquidity (**temporarily**) is a great tool when a good opportunity arises. For example, I have used a RRSP loan with a 6 month deferred payment in August 2011 since the market was down 20% from its April 2011 peak. I knew that my year-end bonus (cashed in January 2012) would be enough to cover the RRSP loan. Since the opportunity was there and I knew that I would invest this money anyway, I used this loan make my investment.

Having a "ready to sell" stocks list: Besides having a "stocks on the radar" list for buying opportunities, you should also have selected stocks that can be sold in your portfolio. While the purpose of a dividend growth portfolio is to keep your stocks as long as possible (since this is the moment that you can truly appreciate the dividend growth power), you sometimes get lucky and make a lot of money with a stock in a very short period of time. If you buy a stock a few months before great unexpected news and the shares jump right after, you know that the stock may have hit another plateau and be surfing on it for a while. So you have the option of cashing a nice dividend in the meantime or... sell this stock and jump onto a better opportunity. I personally always try to select 1 or 2 stocks that I could sell at any time in order to buy a "better" investment. I usually select stocks where I've made an interesting profit in a very short period of time (i.e. when I got lucky enough to buy a stock at the right moment!). It can also be a stock that doesn't show you huge growth over the next 2-3 years and that you know you can buy at a later date for a similar price.

My Favorites Trigger Signals

"By giving us the opinions of the uneducated, journalism keeps us in touch with the ignorance of the community."

-Oscar Wilde

Now that you have the liquidity ready to buy any stocks you want, that doesn't mean you should be in a hurry to do anything. I know people that are sitting on the sidelines for quarters and more. Let's be honest, that's not my style. I'm way too impatient for that ;-). But there are moments when it's easier to be impatient. The good news is that most opportunities on the stock markets are as visible as Boxing Day sales sign on December 26th.

Trust the Media

The funny thing is that while the announcements are usually read, the wording doesn't match with the action you should take. My best source to know if I should be looking at which stocks to buy is definitely the media. When you read word like "crisis", "recession", "high level of debts", "unemployment rates", "Governments problem", etc. You should read only one word "buy, buy, BUY! I'll take what recently happened in 2011 as an example. While the companies are making higher profits than they were back in 2008 (before the crisis), their stocks are well undervalued compared to the same period in time.

After 2008, most companies cut down their costs, improved their productivity and restructured their debt correctly. This is why they are highly profitable and have tons of cash sitting in their bank account. However, this *fact* doesn't reflect the stock value. Why? Because there remains a lot of uncertainty around the Euro zone and the U.S. Government debts. While everybody is scared and worried, nobody figures that most companies don't have problems similar to Governments, and this is why they can go through a potential recession without much harm. These are the moments where you have to remember that you are not buying emotions when you are purchasing a stock. You are buying a company making money. So your only concern should be "will this company continue to make money in the upcoming years?". I guess you won't stop gassing your car, drop your cell phone or cease going to the grocery store in the upcoming years. So I also guess that well managed companies in those fields are pretty safe regardless if the Canadian Government budget shows a deficit, right?

Bad news and stock market panic are usually my favorite triggers to start looking actively for stocks to buy. I do that because I don't have much time to invest in managing my portfolio and the media are fairly reliable to emphasize any panic movement on the market. However, if you are more meticulous and have more time, you can also use the moving average to detect entry point.

Let's take a step back and look at what the moving average represents. The moving average is a statistical concept used to measure major trends in data. The moving average is usually used by technical traders. It helps trigger a buy or a sell action. You can use a moving average with any number of data points you want (10, 20, 30, 50, 100, 200, etc).

Moving Average Example

Let's say that you have 50 data points and you want to calculate the 20 days Moving average. You will take the data from 1 to 20 and make an average. This will be your first point. Then, you will take the data 2 from 21 and make another average. This will be your second point on the graph. You now take data 3 from 22 and so on. Along with your graph from 50 data points, you will also have a smoother line showing the current trend of your data; this is the moving average.

What is the point of using the moving average while trading?

The moving average will replicate the trend of the stock you are following (Evertz Technology (ET) in this example). Therefore, it shows when the stock is on an uptrend or a down trend. As you may know already, there is a huge psychological factor in any stock market. Therefore, if you can predict the trend of a stock or an ETF, you will know when it is the best moment to buy or sell. While this sounds pretty magical, it is far more complex than some wishful thinking. However, the moving average added on the stock chart helps you determine what the major trend is.

How to apply the moving average to my stocks on the radar list?

As the moving average will give you the general trend of a market or a specific stock, the key is to identify the moment where the stock price goes under the value of the moving average and goes back up to cross it upward. If you look at back at the ET graph, you will see that I have circled in red the end of the graph. This is because the stock price is now flirting with the moving average. If the stock rises slightly, this may be the buying signal you are looking for. The moving average will tell you that the stocks should not decrease to a lower level (unless there is other very bad news on the market ;-)).

This technique is not perfect as it can't predict the unpredictable. (Black Swan Law). However, if you have selected solid stocks (thx to your investment criteria!), you will at least buy the stocks at a lower price than if you simply bought the stock the same morning you found it.

Other considerations

Besides the regular metrics such as dividend yield, growth, payout ratio, P/E and ROE, you can also choose stocks based upon other considerations. Once you have your stock on the radar list, you can look for:

✓ Where is the biggest sales growth?
✓ Which company has strong branding or is the leaders in their sector?
✓ Which sector should be more promising in the upcoming year?
✓ Which company has the strongest capital structure (low debt)?

Yeah I know… I'm asking you to think before pulling the trigger. But it's also part of the game to be smart in order to become a wealthy investor!

Don't Lose Your Precious Money - When To Get Rid of a Stock

As a dividend growth investor, you should not be looking to sell your stocks in a hurry. As I have mentioned previously, you should keep your stocks as long as possible in order to benefit from high dividend payouts. But this doesn't mean that you should forget about your stocks once you have picked them simply because you have used a very strict approach before making your investment!

There are a few rules that you can apply in order to follow you portfolio efficiently and not trade under the panic.

Quarterly financial statement – How to not get bored

Each quarter, all public companies must report their earnings and provide their financial statement. In an ideal world, you would have time to follow each earning announcement and read each financial statement. But we both know that you are lazy and that you won't do it.

So here's a quick tip: You can run your ratio analysis 4 times a year (about a month after each quarter... so on February 28th, May 30th, August 30th, November 30th). Why wait so long after the financial quarter finishes? Because companies usually don't disclose their results until before 4-5 weeks AFTER the end of the quarter.

This is how you will be able to see if your stocks keep following your requirements or if they become delinquent. If there is only one metric that is not respected, I strongly suggest that you pull out the financial statement and take look at what happened. A quick look at SEDAR[12] should be enough to get the financial statement you are looking for.

---

[12] http://www.sedar.com/

One of the most important ratios in my opinion while following your portfolio is the dividend payout ratio. If the company starts showing a high payout ratio, you may want to sell it and buy a more conservative company. When you are under 60%, there are definitely no worries. But when you are getting over 75%, the red light should go on and this stock should be on your "stocks to sell" lists. It doesn't mean that you have to sell it right away. But it does mean that you should look for another buying opportunity and make the switch once you have found a better investment.

It is important to read the financial statements while asking yourself "will the company continue to raise its dividend overtime with such results?". If the answer is "no"--- **sell the stock**. You are not in this business to fall in love with a stock; you are in this business to earn continuously growing dividends. If you have a doubt about a company, don't wait until your doubt is 100% confirmed. There are too many great companies that you don't have to carry doubts in your portfolio. You need to carry excellent dividend payers!

Upon each quarterly result, you have the possibility to read the "Earnings Call Transcripts". This is the transcript of the conference the company holds to present its results. If you have doubts about a company, chances are that financial analysts will share some of the same concerns. Throughout the transcripts, you will be able to see which kind of questions they are asking and on which points they are insisting. This should be enough to reassure yourself of keeping the stock or selling it.

Don't mess with dividend cuts

Worse than a high dividend payout ratio (or following the later), there is a dividend cut. This should be an immediate sell as there is no hope for you to build a dividend growth portfolio with stocks cutting their dividends.

However, you should have seen the dividend cut coming and sold the stocks way before that happens. High competition, decreasing sales and revenues growth mixed with an increasing dividend payout ratio should be enough for you to pull the trigger.

Don't get emotional or try to find excuse to a dividend cut. It just isn't worth it. When a company cuts its dividend, you can be sure that they have covered all the other options as it sends a very bad signal to investors. This is simply the point of no return. PERIOD.

Using Stop Loss – The Last Line of Defense

If you are not following your stocks for a long period of time, there is a mechanism that helps prevent you from suffering uncontrollable losses. It is called a stop loss order. A stop loss order is quite simple to understand and to use with any brokerage account. You can use the stop loss order for 2 reasons:

✓ Protect a high and fast gain
✓ Protect your stock from falling down the hole

1st Example:

If you have bought shares of Corus (CJR.B) at $20.22 and the stocks soars to $30 a few months later because of great financial performance, you might want to protect you gain. Therefore, you can put a stop loss at $25 in order to ensure that you will be making at least $4 out of your investment. You need to enter the stop loss in your account:

➢ *You have to select the type of trade (stop loss)*
➢ *The amount that will trigger the sale ($25)*
➢ *The number of shares you want to sell at the price*
➢ *The period (until when this order should be valid)*

If the stock ever hits the price of $25, you will automatically become a seller for the amount of shares you have selected. However, this doesn't mean that you will be selling at $25. In fact, if the stock is falling like a rock (if there is a fraud, for example), you might sell at $24 or $23 depending on the market. Technically, you should be selling at a profit though. The main advantage of such strategy is that it enables you to trade without being in front of your computer when the trigger happens.

2nd Example:

The purpose of this example is to show you how you can protect yourself from an excessive loss. If you have selected very solid stocks, this precaution should not be necessary. However, if you are cheating and playing the cowboy, you may want to protect your portfolio from a more than 10% loss on a specific stock. This is how setting up the stop loss 10% under the price you paid could prevent you from losing all your money on your "stupid" bet. When you cheat on your investment technique, it is always one or the other: a stupid bet or a smart move!

Warning:

While the stop loss is fairly useful as demonstrated, it can be triggered for nothing during a high volatility market. This is why it is important to set a good buffer between the current price and the stop loss.

Consider the fiscal aspect

If you are about to sell a stock in a non-registered portfolio, you should also consider the fiscal aspect of your transaction. For example, if you are about to sell a stock at a loss, check for the perfect time to do so.

If you are in the middle of the year, there is no point of waiting and just triggering your sale right away. After all, if you decide that a stock is no longer fit for your portfolio, you must get rid of it ASAP.

However, if you are in November or December, you might want to determine if you have any capital gains that can be cleared from your tax report by the loss you are about to generate. There are a few rules to consider prior to using capital loss in your tax return:

1. Capital losses can only be claimed on investments within *taxable* investment accounts.
2. Only 50% of capital losses can be claimed.
3. Capital losses can be claimed against **capital gains** in the current year, up to 3 *previous* years or carried forward indefinitely.

Tax loss selling must be made prior to **December 24** of that year (due to the 3 days trade clearing process).

If you don't have capital gains at the moment, you can still generate the capital loss and carry it forward until you have a capital gain. You can also make sure there are no stocks you would like to sell and generate a capital gain before the end of the year.

Tax strategy is as important as your investment strategy!

How Many Stocks is Too Many Stocks?

If you are an experienced investor and have over $100,000 invested in the stock market, it is definitely quite easy for you to have a great diversification and hold many stocks. Then again, you might be tempted to multiply your acquisitions and have 50 stocks in your portfolio. This is called diworsification ;-).

On the other side, if you start your portfolio with as little as $1,000 or $5,000, you might wonder how many stocks you should own. I won't lie to you, at the beginning; you are 100% sure to be over concentrated in a few stocks. But let's look at how you can manage your portfolio depending on the amount you have to invest:

$500 - $5,000: No stocks but...

If you are young and interested in building a solid portfolio, you need to start somewhere. Chances are that you have little to invest and you want to make sure that those first dollars you put on the table will generate income.

If you want to start buying stocks right away, you will incur 2 important risks:

a) Trading fees will eat up your profit
b) You will be over concentrated in a only a few stocks, probably 1 to 4

In Canada, the lowest trading fee you can have in a brokerage account is $4.95 per trade. If you buy a stock with $500, it will cost you $9.90 to close your trade (buy and sell). That is an almost 2% fee that you are paying on your trade. It's not really worth it in my opinion when you can select a dividend ETF or mutual fund with lower MERs that is offering much better diversification.

The second risk is that you don't have diversification at all. If this is your first experience with the stock market, chances are that you will make a mistake. What happen if you have bought Yellow Pages or Sino Forest? Okay, you won't after reading this book since you should have followed my stock picking guidelines in the first chapters ;-). But the point is that you are not sheltered from making a mistake and this could be fatal if you invest all your money in only 1 or 2 stocks.

So until you have at least $5,000 to invest, I suggest you work around dividend ETFs or dividend mutual funds to start building your portfolio. I particularly appreciate dividend mutual funds as they allow you to invest on a periodic basis with no additional cost. We are showing you how to pick the right dividend funds toward the end of this book.

Another advantage of investing through ETF or mutual funds is that you become familiar with the investing world without taking on too much risk. Another great benefit is that you can follow the fund manager moves and look at his biggest holding. This will give you a better idea of how to manage your portfolio.

$5,000 to $25,000: 5 to 10 stocks

In an ideal world, an investor would put at least $1,000 into a stock. In my opinion, this is the minimum required to avoid excessive transaction fees and start building a healthy dividend growth portfolio. So once you have grown your portfolio to $5,000, you can start selling a portion of your dividend ETF or mutual fund and buy your first stock.

I don't think that selling all your funds in one shot is a good idea. Take your time to find great stocks and invest $1,000 at a time. As you grow toward the market of $10,000 and beyond, you can take up to $2,000 to buy a stock. My goal when I trade is to have positions that do not exceed 10% of my portfolio. I sometimes cheat (I told you that cheating could be interesting once in a while ;-)), but each time I do, I take additional risk.

If you can build a portfolio with 10 stocks that are worth between 20 and 25K, you will have a great portfolio started. You can then use DRIP to slowly increase your existing position and continue to put money aside in order to continue your stock shopping. DRIPs will allow you to grow your portfolio at low cost (as reinvesting your dividend will be free!). So before you buy a stock, make sure with your broker to know if it allows DRIPs or not.

Over $25,000

Once you have over $25,000 in your portfolio, you have amassed enough capital to have smaller positions and play down to 4-5% of your portfolio in one stock. I'm not a big believer of having over 20-25 stocks in your portfolio as the more stocks you add , the more time you need to follow those stocks. If you are able to make great selections, 20-25 stocks should be more than enough to provide you with great diversification as well as great dividend payouts.

Trading with a sizeable portfolio is a lot of fun as you feel somewhat "powerful" or have the feeling of being a real trader. However, it doesn't mean that you have to take more risk or that you have to trade more often. In fact, there are several risks you must be aware of when trading with larger amounts:

a) Temptation of trading frequently;
b) The need to buy new stocks;
c) Ignore existing stocks in your portfolio;
d) Increasing your position in one stock in order to try to maximize a larger return.

If you have $50,000 in your brokerage account, you may be tempted to buy anything you see on the stock market just for the sake of making trades. It's normal as you will feel like you are in possession of an unlimited credit card in a shopping mall on Xmas Eve. Each stock you look at will become interesting just because you have the money to buy it. But you should be as careful with your next trade as you were when you had only $5,000 to invest. It's important to keep your stocks on the radar list and only buy stocks when you see a trigger like the stock market going down due to debt instability ;-). So remember: it's not because you have more money that you need to trade more often or that there are more bargains on the street.

Another problem you will face as your investments grow is the lack of time. People are lazy. I am lazy... and I bet so are YOU! So you might do a great deal of research before you buy your stock but you might also be tempted to forget about the stocks and think that they will continue to pay strong dividends. The more stocks you have in your portfolio, the more time you will be required to analyze them and follow them. You should at least look at each of your stock on a yearly basis.

One last point. You have to be careful with the temptation of increasing your position in one stock just because you have more money. For example, if you believe that Enbridge is a good pick and should grow faster than the others, you could decide to put 10% to 15% in this stock and ignore your overall asset allocation. While you will surely do it (I do it too!), it is a big mistake as you are cheating on your investment principles. If you are looking for a solid dividend growth portfolio; forget about hitting a homerun and concentrate instead on steady growing dividend payouts.

What is an Ideal Turnover Rate?

The best trick I can give you if you are looking to become a dividend growth investor is to take a Post-It, write one of the following sentences on it, and then put the Post-It on your computer screen:

"Patience is the Greatest of all Virtues" (Cato the Elder 234BC – 149BC)

Or

"You Seek Dividend Growth, Not Trading Fee Growth, Dumbass!" (Me!)

Or you can write both ;-).

Between your "stocks to sell" list and "stocks to buy" list, there should not be much movement each year. In fact, your stocks on the radar should be bought with additional money (coming from a systematic investment or dividend payouts) and not from selling other stocks that you are "bored with".

If you follow my guidelines on selling stocks in this book, you should not sell more than 10% of your portfolio on a yearly basis. In fact, it's possible that you might not even make one trade in 12 months.

But what if you want to sell 25% of your portfolio in a single year? Well, that probably means:

a) You're not a dividend growth investor
b) You did a lame job choosing your stocks!

Let's put it that way: great companies don't change overnight. If you do your due diligence and select the stock based on solid fundamentals as mentioned in this book; you won't have to sell them 12 months later. When I buy I company, I expect to keep it at least 5 years. Off course, economic data evolves and so does each company---that is why you have to follow your stocks on a quarterly basis. However, unless there is a dividend cut, you should not pull the trigger. You are not a cowboy, you are an investor!

In this type of portfolio, there are very few reasons why you should sell a stock:

a) You get lucky and the stock soared 30% right after you bought it;
b) You found a better investment and made a decent profit from your trade;
c) You see financial metrics downgrading.

As you can see, those are 3 things that should not happen every year. Since the true power of dividend growth is being appreciated after 10 years, it is important to keep your company as long as you can.

Investing in the US Market

« With our technology, with objects, literally three people in a garage can blow away what 200 people at Microsoft can do. Literally can blow it away. Corporate America has a need that is so huge and can save them so much money, or make them so much money, or cost them so much money if they miss it, that they are going to fuel the object revolution. »

~Steve Jobs~

Regardless if you like Americans or not, you have to give them something: they count the most amazing entrepreneurs of all time. And this is exactly why you need to invest in the U.S. market. Investing in Canada is great. You know the market, chances are you know the companies and it feels easier to buy something establish in your country. I get that and I think it is right to do so. However, the Canadian stock market has 2 major issues:

a) It counts for only 3% of the world stock market value;
b) More than 50% of the stock market is formed by Financials and Resources (mostly oil & gas) industry.

Those 2 major issues for an investor mean more volatility and less possibility of obtaining an optimal diversification. *« but the Canadian stock market outperformed the S&P 500 for the past decade! »*. You are right, mind you, gold has kicked all the other asset classes ass for the past decade, but that doesn't mean that you should invest all your money in the yellow metal!

How Can I do it and Why do I have to bother?

Investing in US stocks is quite easy these days as many brokers offer the opportunity to open a U.S. dollar account (for a non-registered account) and you are not limited to 30% of your holdings in international position anymore in the RRSP (this rule has been cancelled). Therefore, you absolutely have no reason holding you back from adding US dividend stocks in your portfolio.

As the Canadian stock market is heavily concentrated in few industries, it is also vulnerable to any economic crisis. As we are currently living in an increasingly uncertain world (and this won't stop for a while), having more stable stocks (such as U.S. ones) will help you create a solid portfolio. On top of that, the U.S. stock markets count numerous dividend growth payers that have been increasing their dividend payouts:

a) For the past 25 years (Dividend Aristocrats[13])(42 companies as of 2011);

b) For the past 5 years and more (Dividend Champions[14])(436 companies as of 2011);

c) By 5% for at least 10 years (Dividend Achievers[15])(191 companies as of 2011).

As you can see, the US dividend stock markets have more stocks than you can even look at to please your dividend investor's fantasies. They provide companies that are well diversified in their product offerings along with their geographical presence (all important U.S. companies are present in the emerging markets for example). They show the strongest history of dividend growth across the world and count on a fearless entrepreneur culture.

---

[13] http://whatisdividend.com/what-are-the-dividend-aristocrats/
[14] http://whatisdividend.com/what-is-a-dividend-champion/
[15] http://whatisdividend.com/what-is-a-dividend-achiever/

Now, Where do I Find my U.S. Dividend Stocks?

Another advantage of buying US stocks is that since the market is more developed, it is much easier to find the information... for free! In order to search the US stock market, I use Fin Viz Stock Screener[16]

It is a free and complete stock screener offering many other options as compared to the TMX (for the Canadian stock market). On top of being free and complete, Fin Viz stock screener is also very easy to use. Each time you select a filter, it turns yellow so you don't have fool around and wonder which filter you applied. The results appear on the very same pages as follows:

---

[16] www.finviz.com

Although it can be difficult, you can easily get 40 stocks to look at. For example, I took the following metrics:

Descriptive:

➤ Dividend yield: over 3%
➤ Fundamental:
➤ P/E Ratio: under 20
➤ EPS Growth next 5 years: over 5%
➤ Return on Equity: over 10%
➤ Forward P/E Ratio: under 20
➤ Sales Growth past 5 years: positive
➤ EPS Growth past 5 years: over 5%
➤ Payout ratio: under 70%

On November, 2012, I got 42 results! The best part is that you can export your searches to an excel spreadsheet:

No.	Ticker	Company	Sector	Industry	Country	Market Cap	P/E	Price	Change	Volume
1	ABT	Abbott Laboratories	Healthcare	Drug Manufacturers - Major	USA	100.10B	15.41	64.35	1.61%	1,482,452
2	ADP	Automatic Data Processing, Inc.	Technology	Business Software & Services	USA	26.40B	19.65	55.97	1.03%	351,236
3	AWR	American States Water Company	Utilities	Water Utilities	USA	832.03M	16.34	42.45	-0.76%	31,644
4	BCH	Banco de Chile	Financial	Foreign Regional Banks	Chile	12.95B	16.47	87.62	-0.46%	9,140
5	BSAC	Banco Santander-Chile	Financial	Money Center Banks	Chile	12.38B	16.02	26.37	-0.39%	330,334
6	CLF	Cliffs Natural Resources Inc.	Basic Materials	Steel & Iron	USA	4.41B	4.84	31.09	0.45%	2,254,522
7	CNK	Cinemark Holdings Inc.	Services	Movie Production, Theaters	USA	2.98B	18.66	26.03	0.42%	80,093
8	DRI	Darden Restaurants, Inc.	Services	Restaurants	USA	6.76B	14.96	53.31	1.41%	256,305
9	ESLT	Elbit Systems Ltd.	Industrial Goods	Aerospace/Defense Products & Services	Israel	1.94B	14.06	36.57	1.95%	2,931
10	GD	General Dynamics Corp.	Industrial Goods	Aerospace/Defense Products & Services	USA	22.72B	9.58	64.72	0.66%	197,140
11	GES	Guess Inc.	Services	Apparel Stores	USA	2.04B	9.53	24.66	1.94%	261,015
12	GIS	General Mills, Inc.	Consumer Goods	Processed & Packaged Goods	USA	26.11B	15.80	40.43	0.42%	662,164
13	GNTX	Gentex Corp.	Consumer Goods	Auto Parts	USA	3.39B	14.31	17.42	4.06%	339,930
14	HAS	Hasbro Inc.	Consumer Goods	Toys & Games	USA	4.90B	14.44	37.93	0.92%	224,044
15	INTC	Intel Corporation	Technology	Semiconductor - Broad Line	USA	96.34B	8.45	19.27	2.12%	17,385,070
16	IATX	Intersections Inc.	Services	Consumer Services	USA	151.03M	7.13	8.73	4.52%	20,536
17	IRS	IRSA Investments and Representations Inc.	Financial	Real Estate Development	Argentina	405.79M	7.61	7.52	-0.40%	21,954
18	JCOM	j2 Global, Inc.	Technology	Internet Software & Services	USA	1.39B	12.39	28.22	0.69%	33,498
19	MAIN	Main Street Capital Corporation	Financial	Diversified Investments	USA	956.13M	9.48	36.02	0.60%	68,882
20	MCD	McDonald's Corp.	Services	Restaurants	USA	86.39B	18.20	86.80	1.01%	

1 2 3 next

Tax concerns resolved!

One of the major concerns for Canadians when buying US stocks is the tax issue. I've personally heard tons of horror stories and I can't even believe that half of them are true. This is why I've been going on and on doing research like there is no tomorrow to see what the truth is about taxes and holding US stocks in your account.

It appears that the answer is quite clear and easy to understand: **you have 3 different answers as you have 3 types of investment accounts:**

a) Registered (RRSP);
b) Non-Registered (cash);
c) Tax-Free Savings Account (TFSA).

What Happens in a RRSP?

Great news for all of us! When you hold US stocks in your RRSP, **there are no withholding taxes** from Uncle Sam. In fact, Canada has a tax treaty with the US government that excludes retirement accounts (such as RRSP and RIF) from being taxed.

Even better, you don't have to do anything with your brokerage firm. When opening an RRSP or a RIF account, your broker will automatically take care of notifying the U.S. government when you purchase U.S. stocks. So all you need to do is login to your account and start trading. Nobody will ever bother you.

This is why it is highly preferable that you hold the majority of your U.S. stocks in a registered account. Please note that there are no maximum amount of U.S. or international investments you can make in the RRSP. There used to be a 30% rule, but it was cancelled a while ago.

Unfortunately, it is not as simple when you are buying the very same U.S. stocks in a non-registered or cash account as well as the TFSA.

Since both types of accounts can be used for purposes other than retirement, you cannot avoid taxes on them. Fortunately, there are ways to minimize the impact...

Taxes in the TFSA???

As I mentioned before, the TFSA doesn't represent a retirement, only accounts in the Canada-US tax treaty; therefore, the normal withholding tax process applies. If you don't do anything after opening your TFSA, you will pay 30% in taxes on US dividend stocks (OMG!!!!).

The good news is that if you fill in a W-8BEN form to declare yourself a Canadian resident, the withholding tax falls to 15% (*you can download the form here: www.irs.gov/pub/irs-pdf/fw8ben.pdf*). By doing so, the only taxes you will have to pay in your TFSA is 15% on the dividend paid. The good news is that after this step, the tax guy will be off your back.

So far, there are no ways to recuperate this withholding tax even though your account is « not taxable ». If you plan to hold your stocks for a long time, the TFSA is still an interesting option as 15% is not the end of the world, right?

If you compare it to holding your stocks in a RRSP, you pay the 15% in taxes upfront but you won't have to pay any more taxes upon withdrawal. If you keep you dividend stocks in a RRSP account, you will eventually pay full taxes upon withdrawal; therefore, if your marginal tax rate is high, paying 15% taxes upfront might worth it as opposed to paying 40%+ upon withdrawal from a RRSP account.

If you are able to maximize both your RRSP and TFSA contribution, you should go for U.S. stocks only in RRSP and Canadian stocks in your TFSA. Note that capital gains are not taxable in both RRSP and TFSA accounts.

Non-Registered Accounts & Tax Implication

So what happens if you buy U.S. stocks in an account other than a RRSP or a RIF? You get dinged by the tax guy! However, the rules are different if you hold the stock in a TFSA or a non-registered account.

Because foreign dividends earned in a non-registered account are not subject to the dividend tax credit & **they are subject to your full marginal tax rate**. As if it wasn't enough and that you don't already feel ripped by the tax guy, chances are that the foreign dividend will be subject to withholding taxes before it lends in your account. So taxes will be taken in the US before the dividend payment is sent and then you will be taxed at your full marginal tax rate. Phew! Is there any place to breathe here or are we just quiting on investing US dividend stocks in a non-registered account?

In fact, while you are obviously way better putting your U.S. dividend stocks in a RRSP or in a TFSA as a second choice, you still get a small tax break by filing your tax return and including a T2209 foreign tax credit form (found online at http://bit.ly/fvCiad). This will allow you to not claim a tax credit on the amount withheld on the other side of the border.

What Pays Best After This Tax Mess???

All right, if I lost you at "hello" during the last section, I'll make it up with this simple chart. I want to illustrate what you will receive in your pocket depending on whether you invest in Canadian or U.S. dividend stocks and in which account you should do your transaction.

So here's a chart where you get the after-tax impact of placing a $100 dividend payment in your investment account:

Type of Dividend / Type of account	Non-Registered	RRSP / RRIF	TFSA
Canadian Dividend	$71.81	$100	$100
US Dividend	$53.59	$100	$85

According to the above chart, you are better off putting 100% of your U.S. stocks in a RRSP and use your Canadian stocks in the RRSP, TFSA and a part in non-registered (if you have a lot of savings!). However, we must add a few notes on this chart so you fully understand its meaning:

#1 Dividend tax credits were applied for Canadian stocks in non-registered account.

#2 Marginal tax rate applied is 2011 Ontario highest tax bracket (46.41%).

#3 I talked about tax implication, but I didn't count that you withdraw money from your RRSP/RRIF. Taxes will have to be paid upon withdrawal (duh!).

#4 The $15 paid in taxes on US stocks held in TFSA are in regards to the Canadian – U.S. tax treaty (once the W-8BEN form filled, your irrecoverable withheld tax drop from 30% to 15%).

The chart looks cool, but you are not convinced of the real impact on your portfolio? Here's an example that will prove how bad it is to have your US stocks elsewhere than your RRSP account:

Let's say you have an investment paying $1,000 in U.S. dividends every year. If you simply cash this dividend payout and there is not a dividend increase, you will receive $11,602.50 more in a RRSP account compared to a cash account.

Years	Non-Registered	RRSP / RRIF	TFSA
1	$535.90	$1,000.00	$850.00
5	$2,679.50	$5,000.00	$4,250.00
10	$5,359.00	$10,000.00	$8,500.00
15	$8,038.50	$15,000.00	$12,750.00
20	$10,718.00	$20,000.00	$17,000.00
25	$13,397.50	$25,000.00	$21,250.00

Even if you factor the tax you will have to pay from the $25,000 to take it off the RRSP account, you are still a winner. In fact, even at a marginal tax rate of 44%, you will end-up being positive (a tax payment of $11,000 will leave you with $14,000 instead of $13,397.50 in your pocket).

Keep in mind that I haven't considered exponential factors that would have brought those numbers to a whole different level. If you consider consistent dividend growth along with a dividend reinvestment over the next 25 years, the difference will be huge.

If I want to be fair, I also need to show you how much you would get if you would invest in a Canadian stock in a non-registered account. If you are investing all your U.S. stocks in the RRSP, chances are that you will have to invest in Canadian stocks for your non-registered investments!

Years	Non-Registered
1	$781.10
5	$3,905.50
10	$7,811.00
15	$11,716.50
20	$15,622.00
25	$19,527.50

As you can see, the difference in term of taxes is very important.. You will receive $6,130 more if you invest your Canadian stocks in a non-registered account compared to U.S. investments.

Calculating Capital gains Tax for US stocks

Now that we have messed around with the dividend tax implication in your portfolio, I will close the tax section by calculating capital gains tax for U.S. stocks (after that, you will not have any excuses left to not trade U.S. stocks!).

The first thing to remember is that **capital gains tax works the same way for both Canadian and U.S. stocks**. This means that if you generate a capital gain in a RRSP or a TFSA with a U.S. dividend stock; no taxes will have to be paid (whoohoo!).

So the only difference lies with when you have a capital gain in a non-registered account. As I just mentioned, it is the same method of calculation:

Buying price x number of shares – Selling price x number of shares = Capital Gain.

However, both prices need to be converted into Canadian Dollar before calculating the taxable capital gain. Here's a quick example:

- Stock: ABC on NYSE

- Buy Price USD: $15 x 100 shares = $1,500

- Buy CAD/USD Exchange: 1.02 (on day of buy trade)

- **Buy CAD: $1,530**

- Sell Price USD: $25 x 100 shares = $2,500

- Sell CAD/USD: 0.92 (on day of sell trade)

- **Sell CAD: $2,300**

- Capital Gain: $770 (minus trading commission)

- Capital Gains Tax: ($770 minus trading commissions) x 50% x marginal tax rate

So while you technically have to generate a capital gain of $1,000 in U.S. dollars, the tax guy will take into consideration that you have to convert this money into Canadian Dollars. In the above example, the CAD lost $0.10 so you are feeling like a wiseass since you are paying less tax (but you are making less money too! Doh!); however, the opposite will also be true:

- Stock: ABC on NYSE

- Buy Price USD: $15 x 100 shares = $1,500

- Buy CAD/USD Exchange: **0.92** (on day of buy trade)

- **Buy CAD**: **$1,380**

- Sell Price USD: $25 x 100 shares = $2,500

- Sell CAD/USD: **1.02** (on day of sell trade)

- **Sell CAD: $2,550**

- Capital Gain: $1,170 (minus trading commission)

- Capital Gains Tax: ($1,170 minus trading commissions) x 50% x marginal tax rate

For the very same transaction, you must generate an additional profit of $400 by converting your money at the "right time." This is why you have to remember that you are not only taxed on the capital gain generated by the stock, but also by the variation of currency.

If you wonder which exchange rate you must use to calculate your transaction, you can rely on the Bank of Canada website[17] showing all the Forex history you need. You just need to pick the exchange rate on the date of the purchase and sale of your stock.

---

[17] http://www.bankofcanada.ca/rates/exchange/can-us-rate-lookup/

Currency risk – One last word of warning before you trade

The last example of taxes on capital gains lead me to the last section of **why you should have some exposure to U.S stocks in your portfolio**. While it's important to know **why**, it's even more important to know **how**.

The U.S. market is an amazing market where you can find plenty of great companies that are well diversified and even open the doors to emerging markets without all the risk involved. However, there is one last thing to consider before trading: regardless of the type of account you are trading (registered, non-registered or TFSA), you are exposed to currency risk.

As you noticed in the last example, the exchange rate between the CAD and USD will make a big difference in your yield. After all, what is the point of raking a 4% US dividend when CAD gains 5% at the end of the year? While the 4% will be consistent throughout the years and increasing, I doubt you will constantly gain 5% over the U.S. dollar year after year. That's why the currency risk should not bother you too much.

Prior to opening your RRSP account with a broker (or trading U.S. stocks in your existing account), do a little research to find out if you can open a **USD RRSP account**. Why is this so important? Because brokers make tons of money from the currency conversion game!

If you want to invest in the U.S. market, you basically have 2 options:

a) Having a CDN$ account where your U.S. holdings will be converted automatically (dividend payouts included);
b) Having a US$ account where your U.S. holdings will be kept in the same currency (dividend payouts included).

The main difference between the 2 is that when the broker receives money for your account (from the sale of a U.S. stock or a dividend payout), it will automatically convert that into Canadian dollars if you don't have a U.S. account. If you want to cash this money or invest it in a Canadian stock, that's fine. However, if you are thinking of buying other U.S. stocks (which should be the case as all of your U.S. stocks should be held in your RRSP), you will be paying some hefty conversion fees.

Consider the following example:

Currency rate is as follows: The broker is buying U.S. dollars at $0.9851 CDN and selling U.S. dollar at $1.0379 (don't laugh, I took these numbers from a Canadian bank website).

You sell 100 shares of KO @ $68.35 USD for $6,835 USD.

The $6,835 USD is then received by the broker who "buys" the U.S. dollar and converts it to your account at a rate of $0.9851. Therefore, you will receive $6733.16 Canadian dollar in your account.

If the same day you buy shares of INTC with your $6,733.16, you will only have $6,487.29 US dollar to make your trade.

Therefore, the conversion process costs you $347.71 U.S. dollar or 5.08% of your investment.

So in split seconds, you just wiped out more than the dividend yield for an entire year simply by selling and buying a U.S. stock! I don't think you want to burn 5% of your money each time you do a U.S. transaction, do you?

Here's the list of brokers and if they offer US$ RRSP account (to the best of my knowledge as of January 2012):

Broker	US$ RRSP
Scotia iTrade	No
Credential Direct	No
TD Waterhouse	No
Qtrade	Yes
National Bank	No
CIBC Investor Edge	No
BMO Investor Line	Yes
RBC Direct	Yes
Questrade	Yes
HSBC	No
Virtual Brokers	Yes
Jitney Trade	Yes

In terms of trading fees and the possibility of having a USD account, Questrade[18] is probably the strongest broker in Canada at the moment. The link to open a Questrade account is an affiliate link but if you look at their trading commission structure ($4.95) and the fact that they are offering USD RRSP account, you will find that I'm not biased ;-).

To Hedge or Not to Hedge – that is the question

Over time, financial theory shows that you don't really need a hedge against the currency you are trading. The fact is that, over time, you will sometimes buy U.S. dollars at a good price and other times you will do so at a bad price (i.e. higher value than the CAD).

The current market we are in right now (2011-2012) is one with parity between the CAD and the U.S. Therefore, you should not be

---

[18] http://www.thefinancialblogger.com/Questrade

too worried about buying U.S. dollars when, historically, the CAD should be valued lower than the U.S. greenback.

Your chances of seeing the U.S. dollar worth $1.10 CAD in a few years is very possible once the economic turbulence is over. Without going into much speculation, let just say that buying at parity is a good move overall.

With a 4% dividend yield if you hold a U.S. stock for 10 years, you will still break even if our dollar gains 40% in value. That is not to take into consideration a dividend increase or capital appreciation (over 10 years, I wish your stock value will grow!). The diversification brought by some U.S. stocks in your portfolio will more than compensate for any currency risk. If you are retired, you might want to reduce your exposure to this risk by selling your U.S. stocks and reverting back into more Canadian bonds, REITs or blue chips. The other option is to buy futures contracts on the Forex. Unfortunately, that is going way beyond the scope of this book. Instead, I'll be covering the "ideal" proportion of U.S. stocks in your portfolio according to different investor profiles in another section.

REITs- The Retirees Best Friend...

"I don't know if I can live on my income or not – the government won't let me try it."

-Bob Thaves

If you have been an active investor since the beginning of the 2000's, you surely remember the Canadian gold mine called Income Trust. Back then, there were many oil & gas companies benefitting from a tax break as long as they distributed most of their income back to its shareholders. This system was almost perfect: you, as an investor, would benefit from the highest dividend yield to support an expanding industry. They, as companies, would benefit from the highest interest for their shares and dispose all the equity they needed to develop their business.

The system was so perfect that many other companies from different sectors jumped in the dance. It was a no brainer, since becoming an income trust would basically means 2 things:

✓ Less taxes to be paid;
✓ More interest for their shares (e.g. more money for stock option holders too!).

After a huge party for investors (from 2000 to 2006, the return on such income trust was too good to be true) the Government came to put a stop to this madness like parents coming back home "too soon" while their teenagers were holding a "quiet evening with a few friends." On October 31st 2006, Canadian Federal Finance Minister Jim Flaherty announced that all income trust would be taxed again under a similar tax rate to corporations as of January 2011. This is how most companies decided to revert back to regular corporations and this was the end of high paying dividend income trusts.

The end? Not exactly... The Real Estate Income Trusts (called REIT's) have been spared from this tax measure. That's why today you still find income trusts in this industry. Since they are paying high distributions, I've decided to include a special section in this book dedicated to REITs. It is important to understand that while REITs are paying great distributions, you can't use the same valuation model that you use for dividend stocks. Here's why...

What are REITs How Do They Work?

First things first, there are 2 types of beasts in this industry:

✓ Mortgage REIT (which makes money out of buying mortgage debts and mortgage-based securities);
✓ Equity REIT (which makes money from operating, developing, selling, renting, real estate).

As the market shows, only 10% of Mortgage REIT and all those security backed mortgage environment are cloudy (remember 2008 anyone?), I'll keep my money away from this segment. On the other hand, equity REITs can be very appealing if you are looking for a steady income.

A REIT is a type of tax structure enabling the company to **not pay taxes** in exchange for distributing a high percentage of its profit to shareholders. To be precise, a REIT must distribute 90% of its profit to shareholders to be considered as such. Therefore, REITs are literally passing their rents to shareholders after keeping a small portion for management and maintenance fees (including interest!).

REITs have basically 3 ways to increase benefits to their shareholders: They can raise their rents, manage the property more efficiently, or buy the right property in order to maximize the growth value of each building. As you can see, these 3 ways are directly dependent on interest rates and the general housing economy. If the rates are low, the cost of borrowing is cheap for REITs and they can easily generate income.

The REIT yield has been **outperforming bonds** while **underperforming stocks**. In other words, REIT represents a higher risk than bonds but a lower risk than stocks. If you are looking to build a 100% stock portfolio, REITs can be a great addition as it won't lower your payouts while providing an additional hedge against volatility. It is also not as correlated to the stock market. This is why I say it's a good match for retirees!

REITs are being traded on the stock market as any other stocks. It allows the "small" investors to participate in the real estate market without having to disburse an important amount, contract a mortgage or spend time managing his asset.

Equity REITs can be active in several markets:

✓ Apartments;
✓ Commercial centers;
✓ Healthcare centers;
✓ Office complexes.

Some REITs are heavily concentrated in a specific sector, while others make the bet on diversification. The same applies with respect to geographic locations.

Why should you care about having REITs in your portfolio?

There are several good reasons why investors are interested in REITs. The most popular reason is probably the high yield, REITs are more than simply the sole income trust survivors in Canada. Let's take a deeper look at all their benefits:

You get exposure to Real Estate without being a landlord. Instead of taking care of your own tenants and answering their demands, you benefit from the joys associated with being the landlord (e.g. reaping rents and growth equity in your property) without suffering from the downside (so you don't have to wake-up at 2am for a leaking toilet bowl!). Many people consider that bricks are more solid than anything. Investing in REITs is a new way to access this asset class without having to include "property management time" in your schedule.

Real Estate brings a great diversification to your portfolio. Research has proved that REITs are not directly correlated to stock market movements. Canadian REITs are known to be diversified and receiving steady income. Therefore, when the stock market dips, REITs won't suffer the same amplitude of loss. One of the biggest reasons is that most investors will keep their shares in order to continue receiving their payouts!

REITs trade like stocks, therefore, it's easy to buy this asset class. There are privately held REITs but they show too many restraint aspects when you can directly trade bigger REITs on the stock market. In a span of a few minutes, you can buy units of any REITs. This is faster than any Real Estate transaction (especially if you need to sell your shares fast for liquidity purposes!).

REITs offer predictable income stream. Prior to 2006, several retirees had over 50% of their nest egg invested in income trust. REITs are now the only asset class offering a steady monthly distribution to its unit shareholder. For someone who's looking to build a pension plan like portfolio, REITs are definitely a great tool to create an interesting income base.

You can benefit from Real Estate growth. In a healthy real estate market, the value of buildings will rise and so will the unit price. Unit holders since 2000 are probably laughing pretty hard as Canadian Real Estate never stopped growing. So on top of receiving rents, you also benefit from the growth value through the price of your units.

Distribution rates are usually higher than most dividend stocks or bonds. Since REITs have to distribute 90% of their revenue, the payout is definitely higher than Government bonds but they can also match (and beat!) dividend and corporate bonds for the same level of risk.

It's the perfect definition of passive income! The REIT environment is more stable than many other business. Most commercial, healthcare and large apartment complexes offer a pretty solid and stable income source without any great surprises. In other words, we are pretty far away from a techno oriented environment! This is how you can enjoy your payout distribution by keeping a sleeping eye on those stocks.

Offers a better diversification option than buying your own real estate (and owning 1 or 2 properties only). If you were to buy your own duplex or triplex, chances are that you would have to inject all your liquidity into a single investment. If you were unlucky enough to pick the wrong investment (tenants from hell, building structure issues, environment changes, etc), your concentration in a single asset would put you at risk.

It's a great inflation hedge. If you are scared about inflation rising in the upcoming years, REITs can offer a great protection against it. Since rent tends to follow inflation, chances are that your distribution will increase accordingly. This is another great advantage for retirees, as they are often a victim of rising inflation throughout the year. If you retire at 60 and receive $45,000 per year with no inflation hedge, the very same $45K might not be sufficient to support your lifestyle at 80 (just think of healthcare costs!).

ROC leads to capital gain. I've mentioned earlier that it would be preferable to hold REITs units in a tax-sheltered account such as a RRSP, TFSA or RESP. However, if you can find Canadian REITs providing a high level of ROC (return of capital), there is some tax optimization to be done in a non-registered account. The ROC distribution is not taxable in hand but will affect your adjusted cost base of the units. Therefore, it will trigger capital gains upon the sale. This is another great way to use a different investment tool to differ taxes over time. So if you have more than one REIT in your portfolio, the strategy is to keep the high interest distribution units in a registered account and find a high ROC distribution REIT for your non-registered account.

Be Careful, There Are No Free Lunches With REITs Either...

So far, I've painted a pretty nice picture of REITs, don't you think? But there is nothing perfect in this world and REITs are not even close to perfection. There are several things you must look out for before considering investing in any REITs:

Be Careful – the Tax guy has an eye on you!

As opposed to dividend stocks, distributions from REITs are mostly considered as income with a portion of return of capital (ROC). Remember that income from REITs is fully taxable while ROC will reduce the average cost of your units (and therefore generate further capital gains). Some REITs also distribute a part of their income as dividends. There are no official rules, and it is important to verify each REIT before making any purchase.

Remember that chances are you will pay higher taxes on REITs distribution than dividend stocks. Therefore, it will be important to include your REITs in your RRSP or TFSA. Holding REITs in a non-registered account will result in much higher taxes.!

Higher cost environment (post 2008). The cost of financing has risen significantly since 2008. It might sound counterintuitive as interest rates for personal consumers have never been so low. However, a 6 billion REIT doesn't go to the branch on the corner of the street to get financing. It usually has to issue bonds at a "commercial rate". This is how cost of financing in this industry has risen because it is considered riskier than it previously was. Prior to 2008, financing was easy to get as banks thought they were able to manage all the risks and still remain well capitalized. Now that the capitalization rules are going toward Basel III, banks will charge a higher interest to finance any commercial activities.

The effect of a higher cost of financing has been amortized by the existing long term debt structure. Most REITs have already secured their lower rates for several years (read 15 to 20). Therefore, the immediate impact on income from a rise in interest rates is minimal. Over time, it will definitely reduce income distribution abilities.

Loss of control. Not being a landlord and not having to deal with tenants from hell is an advantage, if you like to control your investment with a close eye, investing in REITs will be a great deception. The management philosophy as presented to the investor is usually vague. Therefore, you blindly give the power to the management team and your investment return will depend on their ability to deliver.

Higher fluctuation than Real Estate. How can investing in real estate asset classes be more volatile than investing in… Real Estate? The fact that REITs are accessible through the stock market like any other stock is a great advantage, it is also a source of higher fluctuation. Units value will be following stock market trends and you will see those drop in value on your investment statement. Such situations don't happen if you own your triplex, as the only statement you receive is your mortgage statement! The value of your triplex is not assessed on a daily basis as opposed to the price of your REITs units.

It's not bulletproof. The main reason why you should invest in a REIT is because of its stable distribution. That doesn't mean a REIT cannot cut its distribution or that its units won't severely drop in value. A bad investment, rising interest rates, or a bad economy (leading to a high number of bad tenants) could results in some serious financial problems for the company. Remember that REITs have to distribute a minimum of 90% of their revenue. This leaves very little room for mistakes or a volatile real estate market.

We have been spared from any real estate bubble so far in Canada but it doesn't mean that it won't happen in the future. For example, I would not be tempted to look at U.S. REITs at the moment. Always remember that investing in REITs is as risky as investing in dividend stocks. The structure is different, but you still invest in a business!

The Ideal Proportion in my Portfolio is...

While building a dividend growth portfolio, I think that adding Canadian REITs is a very good idea. I would never consider them as safe as bonds (because they are not!), but they can certainly play a similar role in a more aggressive portfolio.

If you are looking to build at 100% stock portfolio, the addition of REITs will be a great tool to reduce the volatility of your portfolio while boosting its distribution yield. You don't have to leave too much money on the table. Since REITs are showing an investment return between that of bonds and the stocks, you will pay a decent price for stability.

As we have a complete section on portfolio building in this book (yeah... you'll have to continue to read further to find out about it ;-)), we won't discuss how much REITs is a good proportion in this section yet. Let's just say that in general, anything from 0% (for more aggressive portfolios) to 30% (retirement oriented portfolios) would be a great mix in your asset allocation.

A REIT is a Different Beast and You'll Have To Tame it

Before you start reading this section, you'll have to forget almost everything you have learned in this book so far. Unfortunately, since the tax structure of a REIT is different than a corporation, the analysis method has to be different too. You can't really look at the dividend payout ratio for example, as that will be huge. It's normal as it is part of the REIT requirement to stay under this tax structure and to distribute at least 90% of its revenue...

What sucks even more about analyzing REIT's is that you will have to rely on data that is not provided in stock screeners, as it is not part of the GAAP (General Accepted Accounting Rules). Funny isn't? If you own REITs already, you'll know what I am talking about: the FFO (Funds from Operations) and AFFO (Adjusted Funds from Operations). So let's start with this one:

FFO & AFFO Less Funny but more useful than LMFAO

The FFO & AFFO are probably the most useful tools to analyze a REIT. Since REITs main reason for existing is the distribution of its revenue, you must look at how healthy this distribution is, right? This is a similar thinking to dividend stock analysis, but with different data.

The main problem when looking at a REIT financial statement is the inclusion of amortization in the calculation of its earning. The amortization concept is a GAAP that allows a company to reduce its income by applying a virtual loss in value to its equipment or buildings. Since REIT's are in the business of owning and managing properties, they show an important amount in amortization that reduces their earnings on paper.

On top of that, in January 2011, the application of International Financial Reporting Standards (IFRS) modified the known definition of net income. In fact, IFRS requires REITs to consider their buildings as "investment properties" in their financial statements. Investment properties allow accountants to use the Fair Market Value model (FMV) in order to reflect the true value of the assets instead of a falsely depreciated asset according to amortization rules. This will help bring ratios closer to the business reality. However, there is already a measure existing that avoids any confusion among investors.

In reality, most properties will gain in value instead of losing value over time. Therefore, this GAAP is mixing your analysis. This is why we are using a different approach by looking at the FFO & AFFO. The AFFO will give you hints on the sustainability of future distributions. In other words, looking at the AFFO is like looking at the company's real profit.

The difference in the FFO and AFFO is the consideration of the capital expenditure. The FFO will consider the company's earnings and add the amortization to have a real look at the company's income flow. It will withdraw the proceeds from property sales in order to show a net income flow. A new approach with the AFFO will go a little bit further by withdrawing capital expenditure to the ladder. This is to ensure the true net income flow from the REITs operations. Since each company will have to spend money in order to maintain and manage its property, it makes sense to include capital expenditures in your calculation. Therefore;

FFO = Earnings + Depreciation (Amortization) – Proceeds from Property Sales

&

AFFO = Earnings + Depreciation (Amortization) – Proceeds from Property Sales – Capital Expenditures

Before you let a big sigh out of your mouth I would ask you to hold your breath a few more seconds. I told you that the AFFO can't be found with a free stock screener such as the TMX[19]. However, **REITs are giving the AFFO in their quarterly financial statements**. Even though it's not a GAAP and you would technically have to calculate it yourself, REITs management teams are well aware that you are looking for this info and therefore provide it to you on a quarterly basis. You can surely waste a few hours trying to calculate AFFO for each REIT yourself... or you can simply get the financial statement and read a few pages to find the information you are looking for ;-).

What do you do with them?

Both FFO and AFFO must be brought down on a per unit basis. You basically have to divide the number by the number of units and compare it to the distribution per unit. Then again, those numbers are provided in the company's financial statement.

Here's a quick example:

Number of units: 100,000

Distribution: $1.00 per units

Earnings: $100,000

Depreciation: $25,000

Proceeds of sales & Capital expenditures: $20,000

AFFO would be:

$100,000 (earnings) + $35,000 (depreciation) - $20,000 (proceeds of sales & capital expenditures) = $105,000

AFFO per unit would be: $1.15 ($105,000/100,000 units)

---

[19] http://tmx.quotemedia.com/screener.php

So if you would have looked at the payout ratio (distribution/earnings), you would have seen a 100% payout ratio. However, if you look at the percentage of distribution on the AFFO, you get an 87% ratio. The company could technically distribute up to $1.15 per units without being cash flow negative but would then show a 115% payout ratio.

The FFO and AFFO per unit should be lower than 100% in order to keep a healthy distribution over time. So the magic number will be high, but should be under 100%. That's normal as REITs are required to distribute most of their income. One thing to consider is that if the REIT is distributing 100% of its cash flow, it leaves very little room for flexibility (unless the company accesses additional financing). However, it is also possible that the number exceeds the 100% mark. So is a 110% distribution rate dramatic? Not at all. Say what?

If the company distributes more than 100% of its AFFO, that means that it distributes more money than it receives. A negative cash flow position could eventually lead to a distribution cut or less attractive overall financial position. This is a similar rationale to the one that we apply on a dividend stocks with a payout ratio over 100%. However, there are 2 situations where a REIT can have a negative cash flow position and still be a good investment:

Consider the amount of units in DRIP. If you take the 2011 Q3 financial statement of RioCan (REI.UN), it shows a 104.5% distribution rate of AFFO. This technically means that the company is distributing more money than its cash flow. RioCan also shows 22.9% of its units to be part of the DRIP (Dividend Reinvestment Plan). Those investors don't receive payouts, but more units on a monthly basis. When considering the distribution net of DRIP as a percentage of AFFO, the company shows a healthy 79.5%. REITs count a lot of investors participating in their DRIP which allows them more flexibility in regards to their liquidity.

Future income growth. If the company recently purchased an important complex, chances are that its distribution percentage will be higher than usual. You will then rely on the management's ability to raise rents and improve profitability of the newer complex. If the future income should be higher due to better management on the recent acquisition, you can tolerate a higher distribution rate. As you can see, analyzing the payout ratio of a REIT incurs a lot more gray areas than dividend stocks!

Loan to value ratio

I have already mentioned this several times so far; REITs are not like regular stocks. Another example is when you consider REITs financing structure. As opposed to many companies or individuals, REITs don't get much benefit from completely paying their mortgages. Instead, they use the equity built in their existing property portfolio in order to extend their business and create value for their unit holders. Therefore, many REITs are overleveraged.

This strategy is great in a prosperous economy, but it is important to make sure that management teams don't go overboard with leveraging. As I have mentioned before, the cost of financing has been rising for REITs since 2008. This means that overleveraged properties will have a hard timing refinancing their mortgage later on.

The use of the loan to value ratio (LTV) is a great tool to analyze the future ability to raise cheap debts for REIT. The LTV is easy to calculate from the financial statement, as you only need 2measures of data:

LVT = Mortgage Amount / FMV of properties

With the new International Reporting Standards in place, it has become easier to calculate the LVT. This ratio will tell you how much the company can seek through refinancing and will also tell you if they can raise debt at a lower rate than their competitors. For example, if Rio Can has an LTV under 50% and Calloway's is at 70%, chances are that Rio Can will raise debt cheaper.

Diversification is darn important

A solid REIT is one that will go through a recession without suffering much harm. In order to do so, it requires solid tenants, a high occupancy rate, and great diversification.

When we talk about diversification for REITs, we talk about:

✓ Different type of tenants (commercial, office, etc);
✓ Different locations (city sizes, provinces).

When looking at the type of tenants, a REIT should look at different economic sectors. This will avoid major downfall if a specific sector is hit by the economy. Retails and grocery stores will always be winning tenants in my opinion, as big franchises are less likely to close all at the same time.

Most REITs will tend to concentrate in a single province to build their core business. This makes sense as they will gain a great expertise in managing according to the province's economy and tax structure. However, since the Canadian economy is well diversified from one coast to the other, it is a great addition to look at more than one province when expanding. For example, as of Q3 2011 financial statement RioCan has 54% of its revenue coming from Ontario (this is their core business). However, they also receive 14.9% from Quebec, 11.3% from Alberta, 5.6% from BC and 10.7% from USA. This represents a great mix between concentrations in a specific market in order to become a leader in a niche while protecting their assets by having about 50% of their revenue coming from other places.

Net Asset Value (NAV) – Another Non GAAP Data

Investing in REIT's differs a lot from investing in other varieties of stocks. The NAV (usually shown by units) can be translated to the equivalent of a Price to Book ratio. You can't do the calculation by using the GAAP once again since the property value won't reflect the FMV. Therefore, what you need to calculate the NAV is:

NAV = Total Property Fair Market Value – Liabilities

Once you divide the NAV by the number of units, you have the equivalent of price to book valuation. In order to get a real use of the NAV, you have to compare it among its industry. After calculating it for a few REITs, you will have a better understanding of if the market is overrating one company compared to another. A lower than industry NAV is considered to be either a risky play or a value play. The AFFO and LVT will tell you which one it is.

Considering the Financing Structure

After looking at the LVT to know if the REITs have leverage potential, another factor to consider is the overall debt structure. You need to look at the current mortgages expiring matched with leases expiring. A great combination would be leases expiring soon (as the company has the ability to increase rents) with long term locked-in mortgage since borrowing rates are still pretty affordable right now.

Another point to look at in the financing structure is the number of units issued on a yearly basis. Most REITs will issue a lot of new units due to their popular DRIP. As issuing more units to pay its shareholders is not a problem over a short term period, an increasing number of units combined with a slow growth will be catastrophic for the shareholders. If the main source of financing is done through issuing new shares, you could go closer to a pyramid scheme business model. The REIT would then issue shares only to turn around and give that money back to existing shareholders. It doesn't sound healthy, does it?

Quick REITs Analysis Guidelines

I know that you don't have all the time in the world and that one of the reasons you purchased this book was to save time. After reading the past few pages on REITs, you may be ready to drop this option and concentrate on dividend stock picking. REITs analysis will require you to look deeper into financial statements since most information you need cannot be taken from the stock screener of financial websites. This is why I'm summarizing the above mentioned guidelines to give you a clear and quick idea of what you should be looking for:

FFO & AFFO under 100% - you are looking for viability

Dividend Yield over 3% - you are looking to get paid

5 Years Dividend Growth positive – you are looking to get paid more

LVT under 65% - a lot of equity means more leverage options and cheap debt

Geographic diversification: 55% of revenue or less by province + preferably a small exposure to USA market (it will bounce back one day or another).

Tenant diversification: less than 5% of revenue by tenants + sector diversification

Financial translation from Stocks to REITs

Still confused about what to track for a stock and what to track for a REIT? Here's a quick "translation chart" that will help you figure out what you should be looking for when searching for a REITs, considering you have a background in investing in stocks.

Stocks	REIT
Earnings	Earnings (Rent + Proceeds from sale)
Price to Book Ratio	NAV
Dividend Payout Ratio	FFO & AFFO
Debt to Equity Ratio	Loan to Value Ratio
Dividend Growth	Same! Yeah!
Growth Potential	Increase of rent, management abilities, future projects
Gross Margin	Occupancy Rate

Start Your Research With a Screener

As previously mentioned, there is a lot of data that won't be published on free financial websites when you are looking for the right REIT. However, that doesn't mean you can't start your search with a screener. If you want to use the TMX stock screener, you can start by using very simple criteria:

Industry: Real Estate

5 Year Annual Growth Rate: >= 0

Current Dividend Yield: > 3%

Stock Screener

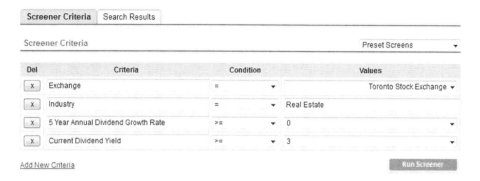

This won't give you the answer you are looking for right away, but it will at least cut the research into a smaller scope already. By downloading their financial statements and looking at the FFO and AFFO per unit, you will probably be able to eliminate a few of them in a heartbeat. The rest will lead you to a few hours of reading and analyzing the big picture...

Portfolio Model According To Account Types

"A man can't be too careful in the choice of his enemies."

-Oscar Wilde

After more than 25,000 words read so far, we are finally getting to the "most" important part of this book: creating your portfolio! What I hate about several investing books is that they often provide great advice, but they always keep it very close to financial theories without getting into the practical advice. I guess authors don't want to be held responsible for wrong advice. Imagine what kind of problems an author would fall into if they advised their readers to invest in a specific way and the readers listened to them carefully and followed through with their investing strategy to the dot... and you are doing this in early 2008. You will definitely want to crucify him or her with rusted nails for giving you such terrible advice!

I'm willing to take the risk, but I'll tell you one thing upfront: **I'm not responsible for your investing returns**. 'Cause if I wanted to be responsible for it, I would charge you a percentage of your assets to manage it... oh wait! That's the broker's job, not mine! So don't bother sending me hate mail if you lose money. By the way, I'm using a very similar portfolio strategy for my own personal account, so I'll be losing money too and I'll be upset too!

So that's why I'm willing to give you my thoughts on how a portfolio should be structured depending on your goal (growth or revenue), your cash (amount to be invested and frequency) and your accounts (registered or not or TFSA).

To make it simple, I chose 2 goals: growth or revenue. If you are seeking growth, it's because you are not afraid of market volatility and you have at least 10 years before you withdraw **all your money**. This means that if you think that your investment account is there to stay for more than 10 years (you do not expect to cash in your investment), you should look at the growth portfolio models. The growth portfolios will focus on both dividend and stock value growth over time and will prefer long term growth as opposed to high dividend payouts. The goal is to spend the next 10, 20, 30 years to build this huge portfolio that will make you feel like Warren Buffett in retirement!

On the other hand, if you are retired already and you are counting on generating revenues out of your book, you should consider the revenue structure. The revenue oriented portfolios are made in a way that you pick safer stocks that will generate less growth, but a stable dividend growth so your withdrawal can follow inflation. One of the major problems retirees have these days is that if they need $30K/year today, they will need $46,815/year in 20 years (assuming a 2.25% inflation rate). In most cases, the portfolio is not built to follow this increase of payment. The ones offered in this book take this point into consideration.

The second important point is the amount of cash you have to build your portfolio. In an ideal world, we would all have 1M$ to build our portfolio and we would all live the good life. You can keep dreaming on or you can go back to reality and look at how much you have to invest. Let's concentrate on that. At the beginning of this book, I've mentioned 3 different investing strategies depending on how much you have to invest at first:

➢ $500 to $5,000
➢ $5,000 to $25,000
➢ $25,000 +

I'll be expanding on those 3 strategies and provide you with 3 growth portfolio models and 1 revenue portfolio model with a 25K+ example. Seriously, if you want to generate revenues from a $15,000 portfolio, you will be disappointed. This won't be called a revenue portfolio; it will be called a pocket change generator portfolio.

The portfolio models will also include which types of accounts you should be investing in (registered, non-registered and TFSA) and how each account should be invested. Therefore, you will find in this section 4 different models (3 growth and 1 revenue), each of them including the 3 types of accounts. To give you an idea of the model examples, here's a quick chart showing you what will be covered:

Amount ($)	Growth	Revenue	RRSP	TFSA	CASH
$500-$5,000	A	C	B	B	C
$5,000-$25,000	A	C	A	B	C
$25,000 +	A	A	A	A	A

A: included in portfolio

B: may be included in your portfolio

C: is not mentioned in this book

Keep in mind that this section ignores completely your risk tolerance and does not include bonds or other fixed income. Those models are based on 100% dividend paying stocks. I include a mix of the following:

➢ Canadian Stocks (duh!)

➢ Canadian REITs (this is where you can find some "fixed income" aspects)

➢ US Stocks (do I really have to tell you why again?)

According to tax implication, the models will follow the following grid for its composition:

Investment	RRSP	TFSA	CASH
Cdn Stocks	B	A	A
Cdn Reits	A	A	B
US Stocks	A	B	C

A: must be prioritized in the account

B: can be included in the account

C: should not be included in the account EVER!

Growth Portfolio $500 to $5,000

Many people will advise that starting with ETFs is the best way to build your nest egg. However, the transaction costs in Canada is too high to buy ETFs with $500 since you will end-up paying 1.98% ($4.95*2/$500) in commission for a buy and sell operation on top of the ETFs management fee. This is why I think that setting up a bi-weekly systematic plan in a dividend fund or an index fund is the best way to build your first $5,000 in your investment account.

I recently got into this debate with one of my friends and here was my final agreement: if I take the recent period of January 2011 to December 31st 2011 and consider 3 investing possibilities: Altamira Canadian Index Fund (NBC814) and iShares S&P/TSX 60 Index fund (XIU) here are the results:

S&P TSX Total Return: -8.71%
NBC814: -9.60% (net of fees)
XIU: -9.08%

If you have invested in the XIU, you will have been done better than the mutual fund. However, you need to consider what you pay in trading commission fees (a minimum of $4.95 at Questrade[20]) and the fact that you can't do bi-weekly systematic investment in XIU while you can do it for free in an index fund. We could argue for a while in the choice of mutual funds over a ETF in a long term strategy, but since your goal is to reach $5,000 and move on to something else, the transaction fee charged on ETFs closed the debate for a short term investment in my opinion.

The bi-weekly systematic plan is essential since you can match your pay check date and create a powerful saving habit. If you are willing to "sacrifice" $100 per pay check, you will get $2,600 in a year and you will reach the second level of investing ($5,000 to $25,000)

---

[20] http://www.thefinancialblogger.com/Questrade

within 2 years. If you are able to put your bonus and future income raise in your investment account, you could jump to level 2 in one year only!

As for the choice of account, I've previously coded both RRSP and TFSA as "orange". This means that you should pick one or the other and stick to it until you have a larger amount to invest. This allows you to avoid being distracted by too many accounts and statements.

How can you make the choice between the RRSP and the TFSA? The answer lies in your marginal tax bracket. Without knowing your situation, I would bet $5 on the TFSA. I assume that if you are just starting to invest, you are probably young and starting your career or still in school. In both cases, chances are that your marginal tax rate is not that high and you don't really have a big incentive to use your RRSP contribution room.

Remember that while your RRSP contribution room accumulates year after year if you don't use it, you can only use this amount once in your life. Therefore, if you invest $1,000 in your RRSP at a marginal tax rate of 28% because you are being paid an "entry level" salary, you won't be able to use that same $1,000 to contribute in 5 years when your marginal tax rate would become 38% because you are making more money. Your contribution of $1,000 will be taken out of your "contribution room" and won't be able to be renewed. The only way to increase your contribution room is by working more years, as 18% of your income (minus if you have a pension plan) is calculated to create it.

This is how a simple choice of account could cost you $100 for each $1,000 invested in money left on the table. To validate what is your marginal tax rate, I use Ernst & Young Tax calculators[21]. It's a free and reliable resource! So in most cases, you should consider the TFSA over the RRSP unless you are already earning a high salary.

---

[21] http://www.ey.com/CA/en/Services/Tax/Tax-Calculators

Now we have determined that you should invest in a mutual fund instead of an ETF. We have also determined that you should invest through a bi-weekly systematic payment plan (a minimum of $100 would be preferable) and that the TFSA is most likely the best type of account you should open. We all know this, but we still don't know which kind of portfolio you should hold, right?

The purpose of your portfolio at this point should be to:

a) Familiarize yourself with the concept of investing in the real world;
b) Accumulate enough money so that you can jump to level 2 and start trading.

I think that starting to invest right away instead of putting money aside in a cash account is better if you have already read a lot about investing. You are ready to take the next step and open your brokerage account to start your investing journey.

I think you are better off to simplify your investing strategy at this point in order to minimize the time spent on your investment and the fees related to your transaction. This is why I have listed only 2 options to accumulate your $5,000:

Option #1: Index mutual funds

There is an easy way to find the mutual fund you are looking for and it is by using yet another free resource: The Globe & Mails Fund Filter[22]. In a very user-friendly process, you can pull out all Canadian index funds tracking Canadian Equities with no loads (= no transaction fees) and MERs less than 1%:

Be careful, the filter will also give you ETFs listed among mutual funds. Besides that, it's a very efficient filter and you can find the mutual funds you are looking for. Speaking of which... what are you looking for, exactly?

Index mutual funds should do 2 things: follow the index and cost a minimum in MERs. Therefore, you don't have to follow tons of metrics before making your choice. You should be looking at the quartile ranking (must be 1 or 2 most of the time) and MERs (the lower, the better). Don't worry; this search won't make you spend much time, as you will soon be choosing from less than 10 index funds, mostly offered by Canadian Banks. Most of them offer a small minimum systematic investment plan in the range of $25 to $50. As I have mentioned previously, you should start with $100 every 2 weeks in order to grow your portfolio rapidly.

The advantage of choosing index mutual funds is that they are well diversified (since they invest in several companies in different sectors) and that they are very cheap and comparable to ETFs.

The major disadvantage is that you are not really investing toward a dividend investing approach at this stage. You are only building cash to move forward. This is why I wanted to give you 2 options.

Option #2: Dividend Mutual Funds

Using the same tool (The Globe & Mail Fund Filter[23]), you can filter through dividend mutual funds by selecting "Canadian Dividend and Income Equity" in the "Growth and Income" asset class section. I then put MER lower than 1.50% to make sure I don't buy an expensive fund and don't forget to select "no loads" to avoid any transaction fees:

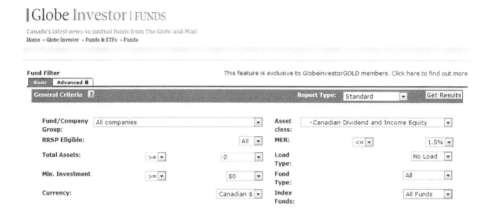

You will get a significantly larger amount of funds to look at (at the beginning of 2012, this filter gave me 64 funds to look at). You can save yourself a lot of trouble by selecting the quartile sheet and transferring this list to Excel. Click at the bottom of the chart and then drag your mouse all the way through and select the whole chart (including chart titles) as shown in the following image:

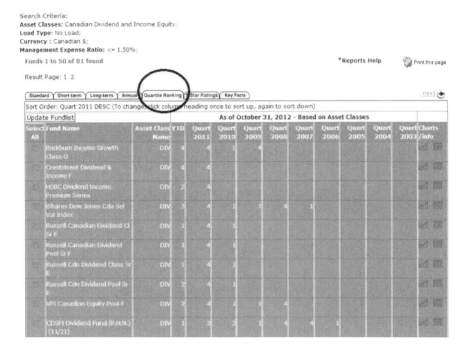

Open   to an Excel spreadsheet and select "paste special" with "Unicode text" option:

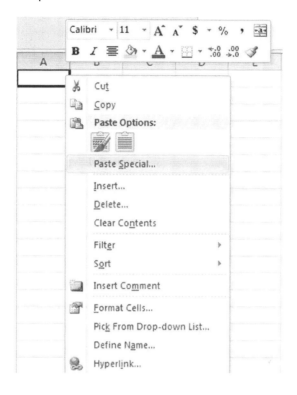

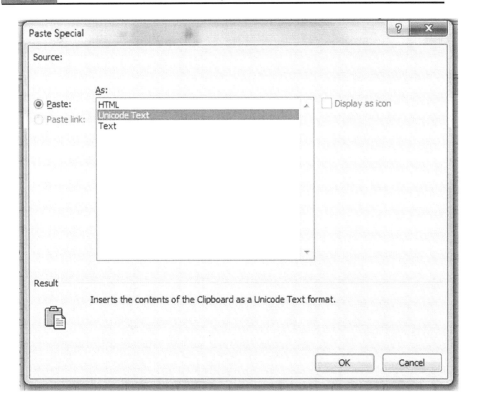

You will then have a little bit of work to arrange the columns, but you will quickly be able to identify the funds that fall in the third and fourth quartile and delete them from your selection. You should be taking a single fund, as your goal is not to build a fund portfolio, but to reach the $5,000 mark ASAP.

In order to be effective, you should put this objective as your main goal for the year. If you focus solely on getting to $5,000, you will be surprised to see how fast you will reach it!

Important notes on mutual funds before we leave

There is a very important thing you must do prior to opening your brokerage account: ask about the fees! Some brokers could charge you to open a brokerage account and trade mutual funds depending on the type of funds and the type of institution. I suggest you call customer support prior to opening your account. This is a small call that can save you big time money!

It is important to remember to be careful about the composition of the dividend fund you select. Some funds include up to 50% of the money invested into bonds instead of dividend stocks. It is important that you seek for dividend stocks and preferred stocks funds.

Growth Portfolio $5,000 to $25,000

Yeah baby! Now we are on to the real stuff: Dividend Growth Investing!

Expanding upon what has been previously written, you should start buying stocks when your portfolio is worth over $5,000. Each stock should not exceed 10% of your portfolio. If you do so, you are taking additional risk each time and your beta will be greatly influenced by 1 or 2 stocks.

At this size, you should already open an RRSP account and continue with your TFSA. The RRSP account will allow you to lurk around U.S. dividend stocks which is great news! If you are still in a low tax bracket, you may want to hold off a little bit and wait until you get a salary increase before you open your RRSP account. The TFSA can easily do the job, but you should not consider including U.S. stocks yet due to tax issues.

In order to build your portfolio, you should not put more than 10% of your portfolio in a single stock. Your goal will then be to reach $10,000 as soon as possible with an average of $1,000 per stock.

As you are probably in the accumulation stage, you should continue (read increase) your bi-weekly systematic plan in the mutual fund of your choice in order to keep building your "liquidity". This fund is your pool where you will get money to buy your stocks. Therefore, each time that you see a stock that is a good pick, you can withdraw between $1,000 and $2,500 (this model supports a maximum of 25K invested) to make your trades.

What happens if your funds return is negative when you want to buy a stock?

Pretty good question, huh? Some might have the reflex to wait until the funds go back to profitability. Others may think that I'm just giving terrible advice and that this money should be invested in a money market fund until you reach the desired level to buy a stock. But I think they are both wrong! Why?

You have to remember your goal: *investing in the market and making money with dividend investing.* This will not be achieved through money market investing! It's being achieved by investing in the stock market.

You might have been taught that you should not sell when you are at a loss. But in this case it's different: *you are selling shares/units invested in the stock market to buy shares in...the stock market!* This is why you are not in a situation of "losing" but more in a situation of "asset reallocation". A bad move would be to withdraw your investment from a losing fund to leave it in cash. But, since you are investing again during the same period, it becomes a zero sum game. On top of that, if the fund you hold is negative, chances are that the stock you will buy is on a slump too. Therefore, you are selling at a cheaper price and buying at a cheaper price.

Consider the following: You are holding shares of BNS for a year. The stock is now down by 5% in your portfolio. After further analysis, you realize that TD would be a better pick and you don't want to over concentrate on the financials (trust me, it's hard to resist, but you must be strong!). What's the problem with selling BNS and buying TD? You are creating a loss with BNS, but your chances of making more with TD are there (unless you are a very bad investor!). This is why you should not be afraid to sell your fund units in order to buy stocks. Follow your investing strategy, not the stock market!

How to start your portfolio

Since we are looking at your portfolio with a growth perspective in mind, I would be tempted to leave the Canadian REITs behind. Those are perfect to stabilize the portfolio (as they are less likely to move as fast as other stocks) and generate a higher income. I don't think that your first picks should include any Canadian REITs.

If you are looking for a "safe" place to start, I would be tempted to start with Canadian Banks or Telecoms. Those 10 stocks (RY, TD, BNS, CM, BMO, NA, BCE, RCI.B, SJR.B, T) represent solid companies with great dividend growth metrics. If you're not considering a bulletproof investment decision, you should not make the mistake of your life by picking   stocks without   a careful analysis using the techniques mentioned in this book.

You should build your "stock on the radar" list and follow them as soon as you are about to reach the $5,000 mark. Once you have your $5,000, you can withdraw $1,000 to $1,500 to make your first trade. If you are hesitating between 2 stocks, call your broker and ask him or her to provide you with a list of stocks that enable DRIPS. Since you want to grow at the lowest cost possible, using DRIPs is the best way to slowly build your portfolio while avoiding high transaction costs.

Adding more stocks to your portfolio

As you continue to invest, you will rapidly reach the mark of $10,000 and over. At this point, you could sell most of your mutual funds to build a 10 stock portfolio. While you continue to invest through your systematic investment into your mutual funds, you will have a "real" dividend portfolio on the side to manage.

If you have decided to keep your TFSA only, you are limited to Canadian stocks (leave the U.S. stocks when you can go into your RRSP). By the time you reach $10,000 in investments, your marginal tax rate should definitely be high enough so that it is worth it to start contributing to your RRSP. This is also when you can consider adding U.S. stocks inside this new account.

As a matter of percentage, a well-diversified portfolio could contain about 40% U.S. stocks and 60% Canadian stocks. As you reach the mark of $25,000, you can consider changing it to 40% U.S., 50% CDN and 10% in a Canadian REITs.

While you are building your investment portfolio through your TFSA and RRSP, you should use both for the same purpose (i.e. retirement) and apply the same investment strategy. Even though you receive a statement separated into 2 accounts, it will be your job to build an excel spreadsheet and combine all your stocks into one portfolio.

Remember that this should be your overall asset allocation and it should not be replicated within each of your accounts. For example, if you have $20,000 to invest with $10,000 in your RRSP and $10,000 in your TFSA, your portfolio should look like:

RRSP Account: $8,000 invested in 3-4 US stocks and $2,000 in a CDN stock.

TFSA Account: $8,000 invested in 3-4 CDN stocks and $2,000 in a CDN REIT.

This would give you 8 to 10 stocks invested with full tax optimization. At this stage, you should not have more than 2 stocks in the same sector since you are starting to have a sizeable portfolio. If you cheat on this part (I do this from time to time), you will be adding more risk to your portfolio. Here's an example of what your portfolio could look like (note: those are not recommendations, you have to work a little bit to build your portfolio!)

Ticker	Sector	Account	Amount	Dividend Yield
CVX-US	Energy	RRSP	$2,000	3.00%
KO-US	Consumer	RRSP	$2,000	2.80%
INTC-US	Techno	RRSP	$2,000	3.30%
MCD-US	Services	RRSP	$2,000	2.80%
NA-TSE	Financial	RRSP	$2,000	4.20%
HSE-TSE	Energy	TFSA	$2,000	4.90%
T-TSE	Telecom	TFSA	$2,000	4.10%
LNF-TSE	Services	TFSA	$2,000	3.10%
CJR.B	Services	TFSA	$2,000	4.70%
REI.UN-TSE	REIT	TFSA	$2,000	5.20%
Total			$20,000	3.81%

The following portfolio gives a healthy 3.81% dividend yield (this is $762/year) with strong companies that will continue increasing their dividends. On top of that, the portfolio is fully tax optimized (U.S. stocks in RRSP only) and well diversified:

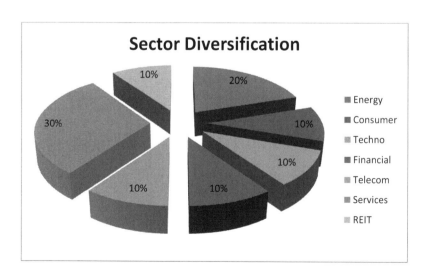

I know that if you are right you will be making more money by picking fewer sectors but let's not start getting greedy here. The more money you have to invest, the more of a "gambler" you may become. This is definitely a risk that will be hurting you for the rest of your life. You are reading this book to build a solid passive income, not to bet your money on the winning horse.

Growth Portfolio $25,000 +

This is where we hit the fun! Once you have a portfolio over 25K, you have an incredible list of opportunities...which could lead you very fast to trading mistakes if you don't calm down and stick to your investing strategy.

Just because you have more money and more trading possibilities doesn't mean that you have to take chances and start cheating all the time from your Jedi Code.

The way to manage your portfolio will greatly depend on how much time you have on hand. If you see that holding 10 stocks is already a pain when you come to your quarterly financial statement reading routine, you might not want to increase the number of holdings. For those who are looking for a less demanding investment strategy, I'm preparing another book on this topic. But for now, we will stick to the dividend growth approach for people who want to invest in dividend stocks only.

As I previously mentioned, the ideal number of stocks in order to maximize your portfolio should be between 20 and 25. Even professional fund managers don't go over this mark. There are many reasons why you want to avoid having more than 25 stocks in your portfolio:

✓ Lack of time to follow all of them.
✓ Cost of transactions to trade and rebalance your portfolio.
✓ You are better off buying an index or a mutual fund that will cover more positions for fewer fees.
✓ Duplication instead of diversification (e.g. buying RY, NA and TD is not diversification!).

Therefore, you are better off holding fewer stocks but taking bigger positions in them. This is why I suggest you start with your 10-12 stocks portfolio (from your $5K to $25K portfolio) and gradually add other stocks until you reach the level of 20 stocks.

As you move forward, setup DRIPs for each of your stocks (allowed by your broker) in order to grow your position naturally. Since your goal is to hold your stock for a long time, buying more shares through the DRIP is a great method for increasing your existing position at smaller cost.

It's not because you have reached a higher level of investment that you should change your portfolio. This is why the proportion of your holdings should remain similar:

➢ 50% of your holdings in Canadian Stocks (mainly in RRSP and TFSA);
➢ 40% of your holdings in US Stocks (all in RRSP);
➢ 10% of your holdings in REITs (in a TFSA).

If you max out your RRSP and TFSA contribution (along with your spouse ;-)), you should hold Canadian stocks and REITs that pay a portion of their payout as ROC (return on capital) in your non-registered account. Among all your stocks, select the one that you hope will reach the highest growth (and eventually generate capital gain) in this account too. Finally, if you are about to cheat (that goes along with the high growth expectations), the non-registered account should be the one privileged. If you miss your homerun, you will be able to use capital loss to offset capital gains in the future. If you hold your "bet" in a registered account, the loss will be… lost forever!

When you add more stocks, make sure to revisit your sector diversification pie chart along with your beta grid. You should consider stocks that are not in a sector you already own. If I continue the example portfolio from the 5K-25K level, I would not add ENB (Enbridge) to this portfolio since I've already selected HSE and CVX that are related to the energy sector. This would put my portfolio at risk for no reason. On the other hand, an addition such as Gamehost (GH-TSE), BCE (BCE-TSE), TD (TD-TSE), IGM Financials (IGM-TSE), Flowers Food (FLO-NYSE), Garmin (GRMN-NASDAQ),

Harris (HRS-NYSE), Johnson & Johnson (JNJ-NYSE) and Procter & Gamble (PG-NYSE) would be a great idea as it reaches different sectors. Note: do not add TD, IGM with a portfolio with NA in it, this would put you in a diworsification position!

As for REITs, I would hold a maximum of 2 as they will surely provide nice dividend payouts, but their capital growth perspective is limited. Since they are already evolving in an optimal market (relatively good economy, very low interest rate and great credit accessibility), I don't see any REITs bursting out like there is no tomorrow on the stock market for the upcoming years.

For example, let's say you have $100,000 to invest. You can build a very solid portfolio earning a 4.16% dividend with 19 stocks:

Ticker	Sector	Account	Amount	Dividend Yield
CVX-US	Energy	RRSP	$6,000	3.00%
KO-US	Consumer, Non-cyclical	RRSP	$4,000	2.80%
INTC-US	Technology	RRSP	$7,000	3.30%
MCD-US	Services	RRSP	$4,000	2.80%
FLO-US	Consumer, Non-cyclical	RRSP	$4,000	3.00%
GRMN-US	Technology	RRSP	$5,000	3.91%
JNJ-US	Healthcare	RRSP	$7,000	3.50%
PFE-US	Healthcare	RRSP	$5,000	4.01%
PG-US	Consumer, Non-cyclical	RRSP	$4,000	3.18%
NA-TSE	Financial	RRSP	$7,000	4.20%
TD-TSE	Financial	RRSP	$6,000	3.52%
HSE-TSE	Energy	RRSP	$6,000	4.90%
T-TSE	Telecom	RRSP	$7,000	4.10%
LNF-TSE	Services	RRSP	$4,000	3.10%
CJR.B	Services	RRSP	$4,000	4.70%
REI.UN-TSE	REIT	TFSA	$5,000	5.20%
GH-TSE	Services	TFSA	$5,000	7.50%
BCE-TSE	Telecom	TFSA	$5,000	5.50%
CUF.UN-TSE	REIT	TFSA	$5,000	6.56%
Total			**$100,000**	**4.16%**

On top of that, you have great diversification:

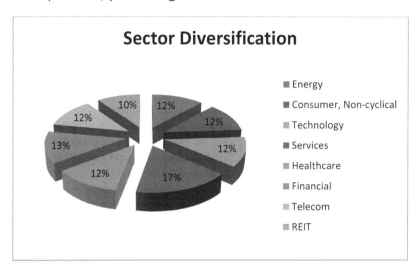

You can also use your newest addition to bring your beta where you want to be (more or less volatile than the stock market). If you are still pretty young and hope for better returns, a strong beta (over 1) is more preferable.

Another point to consider will be where you are at in your life while managing your portfolio. As you are aging, you should cheat less and increase the level of your criteria to select a stock. For example, starting at the age of 55-60, you should start your stock research by using dividend payout under 60% or even 50% to pick only the most reliable dividend payers. Slowly but surely, you will prepare your dividend retirement portfolio with strong stocks that show less growth potential but still comes with a strong dividend payout. The use of lower beta stocks will also be a great help.

Revenue Portfolio $100,000 +

We are now down to our last but not the least portfolio example. The revenue portfolio should be used **for retired people only**. When you get to this level, the game has changed; you benefit from a sizeable portfolio and seek a constant source of revenue. Hopefully, you will have a $500,000+ portfolio to manage at this point because you will need a lot of money to generate an interesting dividend yield. Don't worry, if you have a solid pension plan, chances are that you have under 500K in investment... but your retirement income won't depend on it entirely.

If you have been using the dividend growth approach and kept your stocks for several years, I would not be surprised to see that most of your stocks will generate 5%+ dividend yield at that time. If you consider a stock like KO for example, it has been doubling its dividend every 6.5 years. Therefore, if you buy it now at 2.80%, the very same position should pay you 11.20% in 26 years! If you have not been using this strategy and you are now over 50 and looking to earn dividend for your retirement, you are not too late. Keep in mind that your dividend yield will not be astonishing either.

When you are about to retire, the very first reflex of most investors is to secure their portfolio by selling equities and investing in bonds and certificate of deposits (CDs). It's normal thinking since the last thing you want is to see your nest egg melting faster than ice cream in the microwave. Unfortunately, unless you are filthy rich, going for bonds and CD's will be the worst idea you could have. In fact, the very low yield environment (and believe me, interest rates will continue to suck for a few more years at best) won't provide you with products paying enough for you to maintain your lifestyle. Inflation will eat up all your interest earned and you will remain with nothing at the end of the day.

Step #1 Tame the inflation

I didn't write about inflation sooner because it was pointless. When you are looking for growth, inflation will obviously slow down your portfolio "real value," but your investment return should beat up inflation in a heartbeat. However, when you are retired, you are less inclined to take risks and this is where inflation becomes your worst enemy.

For example, you invest $100,000 in bonds and CD's paying an average yield of 2.5%, while the inflation rate is at 3%. In 10 years, your $100,000 will show a value of $128,008 but the same $100,000 will now worth $134,391. Therefore, you are "short" of $6,383 in terms of value. It's quite impressive for a small 0.5% difference, isn't it? If you factor any tax implications, your difference will be huge and you will be losing a lot of money after 10 years.

When you do your income projection (there are financial advisors that can help you out with that!), you should use an inflation rate of 2.25% in Canada. This is the "magic" number used by most financial planners to do their projections. If you go with bonds and CDs, you will have a hard time covering the impact of inflation after you factor taxes on your investment (or on your RRSP withdrawals). This is why dividend investing is still a great idea.

Even a 2.5% dividend yield is enough to cover the inflation. Say what? Don't worry, you read that right. While a 2.5% interest rate is not enough, a 2.5% dividend yield could be enough for you to cover the inflation. What's the rationale behind this statement? The 2.5% interest rate will provide you with a fixed payment and will remain the same. However, the dividend will increase overtime and cover potential inflation increase, too. By selecting a company that is increasing its dividend by 5% every year, your $1 dividend today will become a $1.63 dividend in 10 years. The same dollar will be the equivalent of $1.34 considering an inflation rate of 3%.

Step #2 Narrow Your Search

I've told you many times that cheating was right sometimes. However, when you are retired, it's not the time to cheat anymore (and I'm not talking only about your spouse ;-)). In order to make sure that your dividend will increase over time to cover inflation, you need to make sure that the company you select has:

a) A sustainable dividend payout;
b) A lot of liquidity;
c) A sustainable dividend payout ratio;
d) Moderate growth perspective.

It's not the time to find potential growth but rather more stability. Dividend Aristocrats should definitely be on the top of your stock radar list. In fact, if you apply a very strict dividend search, you will have to go lurk on the U.S. stock market again to buy interested stocks. But first, your quest on the Canadian market will be difficult as you need to find companies with a dividend payout ratio under 60% and a 5 year dividend growth over 3% to make sure you can beat the inflation over the long run. Unfortunately, those data are not provided in any free stock screen (to my knowledge). This means a lot more digging into financial statements. Subsequently, , it's definitely worth it if you manage a 100K+ portfolio, right?

Step #3 Accept a lower dividend yield

When you are about to retire, your biggest concern should be to protect your investment against the twin dangers of high fluctuation and high inflation. Therefore, you are better off picking up "less risky" stocks and expecting moderate returns. If you prefer stocks that continuously increase their dividend instead of looking at the current dividend yield, you will have a more stable portfolio to get you through your retirement.

I know it's tempting, but it's too late now to become greedy. Now you only need to manage your portfolio according to the dividend payout sustainability over a long period of time. If you started to build this portfolio 10 years prior to retirement (e.g. at 50 if you think retiring at 60), you will be able to combine both high yield and stable stock. This is why dividend investing becomes so interesting over the long run!

Retirement Portfolio Example

Here's an example of a good retirement portfolio which shows more stable stocks with a lower dividend payouts. However, the level of liquidity and payout ratio are much better with this portfolio:

Ticker	Sector	Account	Amount	Dividend Yield
CVX-US	Energy	RRSP	$6,000	3.00%
KO-US	Consumer, Non-cyclical	RRSP	$4,000	2.80%
INTC-US	Technology	RRSP	$4,500	3.30%
MCD-US	Services	RRSP	$4,000	2.80%
FLO-US	Consumer, Non-cyclical	RRSP	$4,000	3.00%
MFST-US	Technology	RRSP	$4,500	2.80%
JNJ-US	Healthcare	RRSP	$7,000	3.50%
WEC-US	Utilities	RRSP	$5,000	3.50%
PG-US	Consumer, Non-cyclical	RRSP	$4,000	3.18%
NA-TSE	Financial	RRSP	$7,000	4.20%
TD-TSE	Financial	RRSP	$6,000	3.52%
COP-US	Energy	RRSP	$6,000	3.70%
T-TSE	Telecom	RRSP	$7,000	4.10%
LNF-TSE	Services	RRSP	$4,000	3.10%
CJR.B	Services	RRSP	$4,000	4.70%
REI.UN-TSE	REIT	TFSA	$6,000	5.20%
BEI.UN-TSE	REIT	TFSA	$6,000	3.45%
BCE-TSE	Telecom	TFSA	$5,000	5.50%
CUF.UN-TSE	REIT	TFSA	$6,000	6.56%
Total			$100,000	3.86%

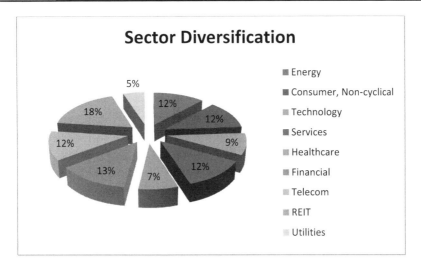

I've started from the Growth Portfolio 100K and modified it to:

➢ Increase the % of REIT as they show strong payouts;
➢ Add utilities as the US market is full of strong paying dividend utilities;
➢ Reduce the US exposition to 49% of the portfolio.

The portfolio model still shows an interesting 3.86% dividend yield while it could be much higher if you would have been holding those stocks for the past 5 or 10 years. This is how your portfolio can really generate revenues.

Investing Resources

"A large income is the best recipe for happiness I ever heard of."

-Jane Austen

If you have read my first eBook on dividend investing, this section will seem pretty familiar to you. However, I'm providing only the "best" resources in this book instead of using too many sources of information.

My Best Dividend Investing Sites

The Dividend Guy Blog – *www.thedividendguyblog.com*

Dividend Stock Analysis – *www.dividendstockanalysis.com*

What is Dividend? – *www.whatisdividend.com*

Canadian Dividend Stock – *www.canadiandividendstock.com*

Dividend Growth Investor – *www.dividendgrowthinvestor.com*

Dividend Monk – *www.dividendmonk.com*

Dividend Ninja – *www.dividendninja.com*

Seeking Alpha – *www.seekingalpha.com*

Sedar (to get your financial statements) – *www.sedar.ca*

Dividend Focused websites

Dividend Achievers – *www.dividendachievers.com*

Dividend Aristocrats – *www.standardandpoors.com/home/en/us*

DRIP Investing – *www.dripinvesting.org/Default.htm*

Dividend Calendar – *www.ilovedividends.com*

Dividend Stock Screeners

TMX Stock Screener – *www.tmx.quotemedia.com/screener.php*

Finviz – Financial Visualization – *www.finviz.com*

Google Finance Stock Screener

www.google.com/finance/stockscreener

Dividend Newsletter

If you are looking to get more information from stock newsletters in order to make better picks, I'd suggest my 3 free newsletters:

The Dividend Guy Blog Newsletter:

http://www.thedividendguyblog.com/2010/11/30/what-is-the-dividend-guy-blog-newsletter/

Dividend Stock Analysis Newsletter:

http://www.dividendstockanalysis.com/dsa-newsletter/

Canadian Dividend Stock Newsletter:

http://canadiandividendstock.com/newsletter/

Ready? Start Your Journey Toward Passive Income!

"Experience is simply the name we give our mistakes."

-Oscar Wilde

That's it! After a six month period of reading, asking my readers what they need and arguing with my partner, you just read everything I know about dividend investing.

But even after all this, you will still make mistakes. I'm making some too! If I wasn't making investing mistakes, I would be charging you a percentage of your assets and would manage them myself... from my boat in the Bahamas!

However, since I've tested this investing approach, I've noticed that my losses are limited whereas the gains are fairly appreciable. For example, I made 28.38% with my trade on INTC in 2011 (excluding dividend yield). All of this to say that yes, you will make mistakes and lose money but you will also have a solid investing approach that will help you make money over time. And at the end of the day, that's the main goal, isn't it?

Patience & rigor are probably the most important words when it comes to dividend investing. But freedom and passive income are the 2 words resulting from it.

If you have any comments or questions, it is my pleasure to discuss my book with you at thefinancialblogger@gmail.com

Best regards,

Mike.
The Dividend Guy

1593286R00078